POINTERS
FROM
NISARGADATTA
MAHARAJ

Also by Ramesh S. Balsekar

EXPLORATIONS INTO THE ETERNAL; FORAYS INTO THE TEACHING OF SRI NISARGADATTA MAHARAJ. 1996 (first published 1987, reprinted 1989) xiv, 261 pages. Paperback.

CONSCIOUSNESS SPEAKS. Recommended both for the newcomer to Advaita (non-duality) and the more knowledgeable student of the subject. 392 pages. Paperback.

EXPERIENCING THE TEACHING. In this book many facets of Advaita are examined and illuminated through a series of 24 dialogues. 142 pages. Paperback.

THE FINAL TRUTH; A GUIDE TO ULTIMATE UNDERSTANDING. Comprehensive and powerful look at Advaita from the arising of I AM to the final dissolution into identification as Pure Consciousness. 240 pages. Paperback.

FROM CONSCIOUSNESS TO CONSCIOUSNESS. This wonderful book explores the heart of the guru/disciple relationship. 80 pages. Paperback.

A DUET OF ONE: THE ASHTAVAKRA GITA DIALOGUE. Here the most beautiful of the Advaitic texts, *The Ashtavakra Gita* is used as a vehicle for an illuminating look at the nature of duality and dualism. 224 pages. Paperback.

Available from

THE ACORN PRESS,
P. O. Box 3279, Durham, NC 27715-3279.
Phone: (919) 471-3842. FAX (919) 477-2622.

(For a list of The Acorn Press books about Sri Nisargadatta Maharaj, see at the end)

POINTERS FROM NISARGADATTA MAHARAJ

Maharaj points to the
Eternal Truth—
that IS before time
ever was

By
RAMESH S. BALSEKAR

Revised and edited by
SUDHAKAR S. DIKSHIT

THE ACORN PRESS
Durham, North Carolina

Published by arrangement with Chetana Pvt. Ltd., Bombay.
First American ed. in hardcover 1983, reprinted 1984, 1987.
First Acorn paperback 1990, reprinted 1995, 1998.

ISBN 0-89386-033-6.
Library of Congress Catalog Card No. 82-71505.

Cover photograph by Jitendra Arya.

Printed in the United States of America.

Preface

I had no intention of writing a book on the teaching of Sri Nisargadatta Maharaj. The material that appears in this volume emerged spontaneously, dictated, in a fine frenzy that surcharged my being, by a compulsive power that could not be denied. There was no alternative but to write, to reduce to a verbal level the abstract comprehension of the Master's words. Actually it was more like listening than writing though my pen apparently formed words and sentences on the paper before me.

When the first piece, now a chapter in this book, was written, I found that my thoughts were running way ahead of the writing. And what I wrote was put away in a folder without even being read over again. I did not then expect that there would be more of such writing let alone as many as fifty-odd pieces. Each time there would be this feeling of compulsion to put in writing a particular topic which Maharaj might have dealt with; and each time the article was put away in the folder without being revised or even read over.

When about fifteen articles had been so collected, a friend of mine, Keki Bunshah of Hong Kong, an ardent fellow devotee, happened to call at my residence. While we were discussing a particular point, I happened to mention that some writing had come about on that very subject only the previous day. Of course Keki, keen as ever, would not let me slip out of what had already been said and was insistent that he be allowed to read the article. Then, of course, he had to read the others too. He then arranged to have them typed, with one copy for himself, of course!

At this time I found myself in a real predicament because I had not mentioned to Maharaj anything about these intuitive writings. In fact I had not said anything about this to anyone, not even to my particular friend and colleague, Saumitra Mullarpattan, who had been doing the translating of Maharaj's talks long before I also was asked by Maharaj to do so. By the time I told Mullarpattan about the intuitive writing and my predicament, the number had increased to about twenty-five. Inspiration for writing seemed to come at irregular intervals of time; I would compulsively dash off five or six pieces at a time and then nothing for a few days.

One morning, after the usual session, Mullarpattan and I were taking Maharaj out for a drive in the car when suddenly Mullarpattan brought up the matter of these articles. He was, like me, aware of the fact that Maharaj generally discouraged his devotees from writing or lecturing on his teaching, presumably for two reasons:

a) the writer concerned might have understood the subject not deeply enough, or he might have understood it only superficially, or might not have really understood it at all, and

b) it might tempt him to establish himself as a pseudo-Gurū and do considerable damage all round.

So, Mullarpattan went about it tactfully, bringing out very clearly that the entire writing was essentially spontaneous and it was not as if I had deliberately sat at a desk with pen and paper to write on specific subjects, and that the very speed with which the words had came pouring out on paper showed that the writing was not contrived. I was sitting in the front seat of the car and Maharaj and Mullarpattan were in the rear. While Mullarpattan was saying all this, there was no vocal reaction of any sort from Maharaj, not a sound! So, with considerable trepidation, I turned round to have a look and found Maharaj completely relaxed, leaning back in the seat, his eyes closed and the most beatific smile on his lips. The message was clear; he already knew about the articles; he had to know. What is more, he was pleased.

When Mullarpattan finished, Maharaj sat up and said,

"Let the articles continue, as many of them as would emerge by themselves. The essential point is spontaneity. Don't persist, don't resist." At this point Mullarpattan suggested that the articles be published, and I put in that they could go under a pseudonym because I was very much aware that I was only an instrument for this writing.

Maharaj at once agreed that they should be published but insisted that the author's name must be clearly mentioned, "although" he added, "I know that you both are aware that all writing originates in consciousness, that there is writing but no authors."

It was a tremendous relief for me that Maharaj now not only knew all about the writing but was greatly pleased about it and had blessed it.

Contents of the book

1. The renderings of Maharaj's teaching in this book are not reproductions from recorded proceedings of the dialogue sessions.

2. They are essentially subjects discussed at the sessions either when Mullarpattan had done the translating and I was present, or when I had done the translating myself.

3. The subject in each chapter has been dealt with in greater depth than would be the case if merely literal English translation of Maharaj's Marathi words at any one session were given. Whilst a substantial portion of a chapter would be what was discussed at a particular session, further material, to make the points clearer and more complete, had to be drawn from other sessions when the same subject had been dealt with. Without this liberty the subject would have lacked the depth which it is hoped it now contains.

4. No translation into another language can possibly convey either the exact meaning or the impact which the actual words of Maharaj in Marathi had at the time. The translation of Maharaj's words in this book is not purely literal, but necessarily contains an interpretation of what seemed clearly implied in the imaginative, forceful, sometimes

terse but virile use of the Marathi words by Maharaj.

5. The reader may feel that I could have avoided the repetitions of many of Maharaj's words, which occur again and again in the various chapters. But such repetitions could not be avoided because

   a) repetitions are what Maharaj calls hammer-blows at the tremendous conditioning that has taken place and which makes individuals identify themselves as separate entities and which prevents the seeing of the Truth; and

   b) Maharaj wants us to remember always that we should not allow ourselves to be entangled in the branches and forget the root; that it is for this reason that he brings us back to the root and the source again and again, repeatedly: "What were you before you were 'born'?" and, also because,

   c) these pieces *are not expected to be read continuously* at a stretch like a work of fiction, and each piece is intended to be complete in itself.

Here I may also refer to Maharaj's oft-made assertion, that the clear understanding in depth of even a single statement of his would lead to an apperception of the whole Truth. Along with this must also be remembered his oft-repeated warning that any apperception of the Truth is valid only when the apperception itself disappears, that is to say, only when the seeker himself disappears as an entity. Any knowledge can be acquired, he says, only in consciousness, and consciousness itself must be realized as being only a concept. In other words, the basis of all 'knowledge' is a concept!

It seemed necessary to include in this volume a short biographical note about Maharaj but, on second thoughts, I dropped the idea. This was not only because the known events of Maharaj's simple and straightforward life are too meagre to write about, but essentially because Maharaj himself had been averse to it, "This is dead matter — as dead as the ashes of a burnt-out fire. I am not interested in it. Why should you be?" This is how he rejected any enquiry about his past. "Is there any past at all?" he would ask. "Instead of wasting your time in such useless pursuits, why don't you go to the root of the matter and enquire into the nature of Time itself? If you do so, you will find that Time has no substance as such; it is only a concept."

Before concluding this prefatory note I would express my gratitude to my friend Keki Bunshah who, after reading the first few pieces, almost pursued me with his affectionate demand for copies of further writing, and to another fellow-devotee P. D. Kasbekar, I.A.S. former Chief Secretary to the Government of Maharashtra, for making certain helpful suggestions. I am particularly grateful to my dear friend Saumitra Mullarpattan, who not only broached the subject to Maharaj and secured for me his gracious blessings for the book, but also encouraged me constantly with his constructive comments as the manuscript progressed.

My special thanks are due to Sudhakar S. Dikshit, whose critical reading of the manuscript in its final stage led to quite a few improvements. Dikshit, an ardent admirer of Maharaj's teaching, heads the publishing house of Chetana, publishers of *I Am That*. When he came to know that I had written something about Maharaj, he approached me and, after a mere glance at the manuscript, offered to publish it. I am happy that my MS is in most competent hands, for Dikshit's editorial experience and expertise as a publisher, specially in the particular field of philosophy, is indeed vast and is internationally known and accepted.

Ramesh S. Balsekar

Bombay
February 1982

Editor's Note

Discovering a new author of genuine merit is like discovering a new planet or star in the limitless expanse of the heaven. As I write these lines I can imagine what William Herschel may have felt like when he discovered Uranus.

Ramesh S. Balsekar, the author of this work, is a new luminary of scintillating splendour that has blazoned forth on the mysterious firmament of esoteric writing of great significance, though himself quite indifferent to his own resplendence. When, after a cursory glance at a few chapters of his MS, which a mutual friend brought to me, I met him and told him how greatly impressed I was, he stared blankly at me. I am no author, he said, and what I wrote is not for publication, but for a clear comprehension of my Master's teaching for myself, for my better guidance and my own pleasure. It was difficult to convince him that what he wrote for his pleasure could profit thousands of others, if it were published as a book. He listened to me without answering — an enigmatic smile on his lips, his attitude affable, but totally non-committal.

Apparently in his sixties and very well-maintained for his years, Balsekar is fair complexioned, quite handsome and amiable, but rather taciturn by nature. When he chooses to talk, he speaks with a circumspection and remoteness befitting a bank president conversing with a borrower. Later, I was quite intrigued to learn that he actually had been a banker and had retired as the highest executive of one of the premier banks in India.

Evidently, as a borrower I proved quite a tenacious person, for I succeeded in borrowing from Balsekar his MS for a

few days for my personal enlightenment as an admirer of
Maharaj's teaching. And as I read through I found it beyond
my best expectations. I lost no time in calling on him and
offered to publish the work. After a brief silence and rather
unconcernedly, he nodded his acquiesence.

I read through the MS again, very carefully, as a deeply
interested reader, keeping my editorial proclivities in the
background. And while reading it I experienced in a flash,
momentarily, my true identity, as different from what I think
I am, or what I appear to be. I had never had such an
experience before. A few years ago, when I had the good
fortune of editing and publishing Sri Nisargadatta Maharaj's
conversations, entitled *I Am That*, I did feel the impact of his
creative originality and Socratic reasoning, but did not have
even a fleeting glimpse of Truth or Reality or of my true
entity, as now. And this, because Balsekar in his writing does
not merely repeat the words spoken by Maharaj, but he
interprets them with deep insight and lucidity and a profound understanding. He writes with a power and an intrin-
sic authority derived from Maharaj himself, as it were. He
does not argue; he announces. His assertions are of the
nature of pronouncements on behalf of the Master.

I never was a regular visitor to Maharaj, but I did attend his
talks quite often, whenever my preoccupations allowed me
spare time. A dedicated devotee of Maharaj, named Saumitra
Mullarpattan, who is equally well-versed in Marathi and
English, used to act as an interpreter. On a couple of occasions, however, I found a person unknown to me doing the
interpreting and I was struck by the authoritative tone in
which he conveyed Maharaj's answers to questioners. He sat
with his eyes closed and flashed out Maharaj's words of
wisdom with a finality characteristic of the Master. It was as
if Maharaj himself was speaking in English, for a change.

On enquiring I was told that the interpreter was a new
devotee of Maharaj, named Balsekar. At the end of the session, when people were dispersing, I introduced myself to
him and praised him for his excellent translation of
Maharaj's spoken word. But he was unresponsive, as if he

had not heard me at all. Taken aback by his intractable attitude I moved away and never thought of him till I met him recently in connection with this book. And now I realize how deplorably wrong I was in forming my judgement about him. It should have occurred to me that he lived on a different level of existence, which was beyond the reaches of praise and blame. I should have understood that he was at one with the Master and nothing else mattered to him. And that it was so is proved by his present work in which we find Maharaj's presence on every page — his exceptional mental agility, his rigorous logical conclusions, his total thinking, his complete identity with the unicity that appears as diversity.

It is interesting to note that in his Preface to the book Balsekar almost disowns its authorship. He says that the material that appears in this volume emerged spontaneously, dictated in a fine frenzy that surcharged his being, by a compulsive power that could not be denied. I believe his statement. And I am inclined to think that the reader as he reads through, will agree with me. For there is nothing in this work that may be taken as the author's self-projection, no improvisations, no learned quotations from the scriptures; there are no borrowed plumes of any kind. The thoughts propounded by Balsekar bear the silent signatures of the Master. They seem to come forth from a luminous knowledge, a swelling glory of Truth that fills his within.

This work, entitled *Pointers from Nisargadatta Maharaj*, is Maharaj himself out and out. It is indeed a sort of postgraduation course for the reader who has already imbibed what is offered in *I Am That*. It comprises the final teaching of the Master at its sublimest and goes far beyond what he taught in earlier years. I venture to say that there really can be no knowledge higher than what this book contains. I also venture to say that none except Balsekar could have expounded this knowledge, for not one of those who have been close to Maharaj has understood his teaching so profoundly as Balsekar.

Some of the devotees of Maharaj known to me have attended his talks for twenty years or more, but their psyche had not altered and they continue to be the same entities they were two decades ago. Balsekar's personal association with Maharaj, on the other hand, extended over a period of barely three years. But such associations are not to be measured in time, if they could be measured at all. What is more important than the length of association is the special type of receptivity that is the forte of Balsekar. I have no doubt that the mantle of Maharaj has fallen on his shoulders. For want of a better expression, I may even say that Balsekar is the living alter ego of Maharaj, though he has no inclination at all to play the role of a teacher. That he is saturated with the Jnāna imparted by the Master is more than evident from this book. But, I draw the reader's particular attention to his special article entitled, 'The Core of the Teaching' expounding in all its facets the unique philosophy of Maharaj (Appendix I) as well as his note on the confoundingly difficult subject of Consciousness (Appendix II). No reader should miss reading these.

Before I close, I may as well relate an amusing incident in which the editor in me had a clash with the author in Balsekar. His remoteness and unconcern always irked me. He is a graduate of London University and has a good command over English. I could not easily find fault with his language. Still I tried to improve his diction and expression here and there, as an editor must do! He noticed the uncalled for 'improvements' and kept quiet with his usual indifference. It was clear that he had made a virtue of his taciturnity, just as I had made a virtue of my verbosity. We were at antipodes, I felt. Longing for a rapport with him, I wanted to draw him out of his shell, anyhow. I hit upon a device. I attacked his exposition of one of the aspects of Maharaj's teaching (though I really agreed with it) and he exploded suddenly. His counter-attack was devastating and I was glad that the shell was broken at last. He was, however, quickly pacified when I agreed with him without much ado. And his eyes beamed with friendliness. The habitual circumspection and remoteness disappeared, giving place to a new togetherness between us. After that we worked together on the book; in fact he allowed me all liberties with his MS and never bothered to look at the additions or alterations I chose to make. We developed the much-needed rapport between us, which indeed I prize greatly. He glanced rather casually at the final copy matter before it was sent to the press and seemed to be quite happy with it.

I asked him if he would write for us another book about the Master's teaching. He smiled faintly and perhaps there was an imperceptible nodding of his head.

Sudhakar S. Dikshit
Editor

Bombay
March, 1982

Contents

Pride of Achievement

"I have worked hard and I now consider myself a very successful man. I would be a hypocrite if I did not admit that I have a considerable amount of satisfaction and, yes, a certain amount of pride too in my achievement. Would that be wrong?"

One evening a foreign visitor addressed Sri Nisargadatta Maharaj with these words. He was in his mid forties — smug, self-confident and a bit aggressive. Conversation then proceeded along the following lines:

Maharaj: Before we consider what is 'right' and what is 'wrong', please tell me who is asking this question.

Visitor: (A bit startled) Why, 'me', of course.

M: And who is that?

V: Me. This 'me', who is sitting in front of you.

M: And you think that that is you?

V: You see me. I see myself. Where is the doubt?

M: You mean this object that is before me? What is your earliest recollection of this object that you think you are. Think as far back as you can.

V: (After a minute or two) The earliest recollection would perhaps be of being caressed and cuddled by my mother.

M: You mean, as a tiny infant. Would you say that the successful man of today is the same helpless infant, or is it someone else?

V: It is undoubtedly the same

M: Good. Now, if you think further back, would you agree that this infant, which you can recollect, is the same baby that was born to your mother, that was once too helpless even to realize what was happening when its little body was going through its natural physical functions, and could only cry when it was hungry or in pain?

V: Yes, I was that baby.

M: And before the baby acquired its body and was delivered what were you?

V: I don't understand.

M: You do understand. Think. What happened in your mother's womb? What was developing into a body with bones, blood, marrow, muscles etc., over a period of nine months? Was it not a male sperm cell that combined with ovum in the female womb thus beginning a new life and, in the process, going through numerous hazards? Who guarded this new life during this period of hazards? Is it not that very infinitesimally tiny sperm cell which is now so proud of his achievements? And who asked particularly for *you*? Your mother? Your father? Did they particularly want *you* for a son? Did you have anything to do with being born to these particular parents?

V: I am afraid, I really haven't thought along these lines.

M: Exactly. Do think along these lines. Then perhaps you will have some idea of your true identity. Thereafter, consider if you could possibly be proud of what you have 'achieved'.

V: I think, I begin to understand what you are driving at.

M: If you go deeper into the matter, you will realize that the source of the body — the male sperm and the female ovum — is in itself the essence of food consumed by the parents; that the physical form is made of, and fed by, the five elements constituting the food; and also that quite often the body of one creature does become the food for another creature

V: But, surely, I, as such, must be something other than this food-body.

M: Indeed you are, but not some 'thing'. Find out what it is that gives sentience to a sentient being, that without which you would not even know that you exist, let alone the world outside. And finally, go deeper yet and examine if this beingness, this consciousness itself is not time-bound.

V: I shall certainly go into the various questions you have raised, although I must confess that I have never explored these areas before, and I feel almost giddy in my ignorance of the new spheres you have opened up before me. I will come and see you again, sir.

M: You are always welcome. ••

2

Consciousness, the Only 'Capital'

Maharaj often comes out with the statement that consciousness is the only 'capital' that a sentient being is born with. This, he says, is the apparent position. The real situation, however, is that what is born is consciousness, which needs an organism to manifest itself in, and that organism is the physical body.

What is it that gives sentience — capacity to feel sensations, to respond to stimuli — to a sentient being? What is it that distinguishes a person who is alive from the one who is dead? It is, of course, the *sense of being*, the knowledge of being present, consciousness, the activizing spirit which animates the physical construct of the body.

It is consciousness indeed that manifests itself in individual forms and gives them apparent existence. In human beings through such manifestation arises the concept of a separate 'I'. In each individual the Absolute gets reflected as awareness, and thus pure Awareness becomes self-awareness, or consciousness.

The objective universe is in continuous flux, constantly projecting and dissolving innumerable forms. Whenever a form is created and is infused with life (Prāṇa), consciousness (Chetanā) appears, simultaneously and automatically, by the reflection of the Absolute Awareness in matter. Consciousness, it must be clearly understood, is a reflection of the Absolute against the surface of matter, bringing about a sense of duality. As different from it, pure Awareness, the Absolute state, is without beginning and end, without the need of any support other than itself. Awareness becomes consciousness only when it has an object to reflect against. Between pure Awareness and awareness reflected as consciousness, says Maharaj, there is a gap which the mind cannot cross. Reflection of the sun in a drop of dew is not the sun!

Manifested consciousness is time-bound inasmuch as it disappears as soon as the physical construct it inhabits comes to an end. Nevertheless, according to Maharaj, it is the only 'capital' a sentient being is born with. And manifested consciousness being his only connection with the Absolute, it becomes the only instrument by which the sentient being can hope to get an illusory liberation from the 'individual' he believes himself to be. By being one with his consciousness and treating it as his Ātmā, his God, he can hope to attain what he thinks as the unattainable.

What is the actual substance of this animating consciousness? Obviously, it must be physical material because in absence of the physical form it cannot survive. Manifested consciousness can exist only as long as its abode, the body, is kept in a sound and habitable condition. Although consciousness is a reflection of the Absolute, it is time-bound and can be sustained only by the food material, comprising the five elements, that the physical body is.

Consciousness resides in a healthy body and abandons it when it is decayed and moribund. Reflection of the sun can be seen only in a clear dew drop, not in a muddy one.

Maharaj often says that we can observe the nature and function of consciousness in our daily routine of sleeping, dreaming and waking states. In deep sleep consciousness retires into a state of repose, as it were. When consciousness is absent, there is no sense of one's existence or presence, let alone the existence of the world and its inhabitants, or of any ideas of bondage and liberation. This is so because the very concept of 'I' is absent. In the dream state a speck of consciousness begins to stir — one is not yet fully awake — and then in a split-second, in that speck of consciousness is created an entire world of mountains and valleys, rivers and lakes, cities and villages with buildings and people of various ages, *including the dreamer himself*. And, what is more important, the dreamer has no control over what the dreamed figures are doing! In other words, a new living world is created in a split-second, fabricated out of memory and imagination merely by a single movement in that speck of consciousness. Imagine, therefore, says Maharaj, the extraordinary power of this consciousness, a mere speck of which can contain and project an entire universe. When the dreamer wakes up, the dream-world and the dreamed figures disappear.

What happens when the deep sleep as also the dream state are over and consciousness appears again? The *immediate* sense then is that of existence and presence, not the presence of 'me' but presence as such. Soon, however, the mind takes over and creates the 'I' - concept and awareness of the body.

Maharaj tells us repeatedly that we are so accustomed to thinking of ourselves as bodies having consciousness, that we find it very difficult to accept or even understand the real position. Actually it is consciousness which manifests itself in innumerable bodies. It is, therefore, essential to apperceive that birth and death are nothing but the beginning and the ending of a stream of movements in consciousness, interpreted as events in space-time. If we can realize this, we shall also realize that we are pure being-awareness-bliss in our original pristine state, and when in touch with consciousness, we are only the witnessing of (and totally apart from) the various movements in consciousness. This is an indisputable fact, because obviously, *we cannot be what we perceive; the perceiver must be different from what he perceives.*   ●●

3

In Face of Death

Visitor: My only son died a few days ago in a car accident, and I find it almost impossible to accept his death with a philosophic fortitude. I know that I am not the first person to suffer such bereavement. I also know that each one of us has to die some time. I have in my mind sought solace from all the usual ploys by which one consoles oneself and others in such predicaments. And yet, I come back to the tragic fact that a cruel fate should deprive my son of everything in the prime of his life. Why? Why? I keep on asking myself. Sir, I cannot get over my grief.

Maharaj: (After sitting for a minute or so, with his eyes closed) It is unavailing and futile to say that I am grieved because in the absence of 'self' ('me' as an individual) there are no 'others', and I see myself mirrored in all of you. Obviously, you have not come to me for mere sympathy, which you surely must have received in abundance from your relatives and friends. Remember, one goes through life, year after year, enjoying the usual pleasures and suffering the usual pains, but never once seeing life in its true perspective. And what is the true perspective? It is this: *There is no 'me', nor 'you'; there never could be any such entities.* Every man should understand this and have the courage to live his life with this understanding.

Do you have this courage, my friend? Or, must you wallow in what you call your grief?

V: Maharaj, pardon me, I do not fully understand what you have said, but I do feel startled and shaken. You have exposed the core of my being, and what you have said so pithily appears to be the golden key to life. Please elaborate on what you have just said. What exactly is it that I must do?

M: Do? Do? Absolutely nothing: Just see the transient as transient, the unreal as unreal, the false as false, and you will realize your true nature. You have mentioned your grief. Have you ever looked at 'grief' in the face and tried to understand what it really is?

To lose somebody or something you have loved dearly, is bound to cause sorrow. And since death is total annihilation with absolute finality, the sorrow caused by it is unmitigated. But even this overwhelming sorrow can not last long, if you intellectually analyze it. What exactly are you grieving for? Go back to the beginning: Did you and your wife make any agreement with someone that you would have a son — a particular body — and that he would have a particular destiny? Is it not a fact that his conception itself was a chance? That the foetus survived the many hazards in the womb was another matter of chance. That the baby was a boy was yet another chance. In other words what you called your 'son' was just a chance event, a happening over which you have had no control at all at any time, and now that event has come to an end.

What exactly are you grieving for? Are you grieving for the few pleasant experiences and the many painful experiences that your son has missed in the years to come? Or, are you, really and truly, grieving for the pleasures and conveniences that you will no longer be able to receive from him?

Mind you, all this is from the point of view of the false! Nonetheless, are you with me so far?

V: I am afraid, I continue to remain stunned. I certainly follow what you have just said. Only, what did you mean when you said that all this was on the level of the false?

M: Ah! Now we shall come to the truth. Please understand as truth, that you are not an individual, a 'person'. The person, that one thinks one is, is only a product of imagination and the self is the victim of this illusion. 'Person' cannot exist in its own right. It is the self, consciousness, that mistakenly believes that there is a person and is conscious of being it. Change your viewpoint. Don't look at the world as something outside of yourself. See the person you imagine yourself to be as a part of the world — really a dream-world — which you perceive as an appearance in your consciousness, and look at the whole show from the outside. Remember, you are not the mind, which is nothing but the content of consciousness. As long as you identify yourself with the body-mind you are vulnerable to sorrow and suffering. *Outside the mind there is just being, not being father or son, this or that.*

You are beyond time and space, in contact with them only at the point of now and here, but otherwise timeless, spaceless and invulnerable to any experience. Understand this and grieve no more. Once you realize that there is nothing in this world that you can or need call your own, you will look at it from the outside, as you look at a play on the stage or a movie on the screen, admiring and enjoying, perhaps suffering, but deep down, quite unmoved.   ●●

4

Manifest and the Unmanifest are One

Is 'I' an ever-present entity appearing at different levels — manifest and un-manifest? This question is often posed before Maharaj in various ways, in different words, by different persons, the essence of the question being the same. Sometimes the bolder visitor might bring up the question right at the start of a session, if Maharaj should happen to mention, which he often does, that his listeners must always bear in mind that he is talking not as an individual to another individual, but as consciousness to consciousness about the nature of consciousness.

According to Maharaj, at the level of the mind, the 'I' may be considered under three aspects: 1. The impersonal — Avyakta (un-manifest), the Absolute 'I', beyond all sensory perception or experience and unaware of itself. 2. The super-personal — Vyakta (manifested), which is the reflection of the Absolute in consciousness, as 'I am', and 3. the personal — Vyakti, which is a construct of the physical and vital processes, the psychosomatic apparatus in which consciousness manifests itself.

Maharaj, however, makes it a point to repeat at frequent intervals, that such distinction is purely a notional one, and cannot exist in reality. Essentially there is no difference between the manifest (Vyakta) and the un-manifest (Avyakta), just as there is no difference essentially between light and daylight. The universe is full of light but that light cannot be seen until it is reflected against a surface as daylight; and what the daylight reveals is the individual person (Vyakti). The individual in the form of the human body is always the object; consciousness (as the witnessing) is the subject, and their relation of mutual dependence (consciousness cannot appear without the apparatus of a body and the body cannot have sentience without consciousness) is the proof of their basic identity with the Absolute. They both are the same consciousness; one at rest, the other in movement — each conscious of the other.

The entire manifested universe, explains Maharaj, exists only in consciousness. The conceptualized process would be as follows: Consciousness arises in Pure Being, for no particular cause or reason other than that it is its nature to do so — like waves on the surface of the sea. In consciousness the world appears and disappears; and each one of us is entitled to say: All there is, is I, all there is, is mine; before all beginnings, after all endings, I am there to witness whatever happens. *'Me', 'you' and 'he' are only appearances in consciousness — all are basically 'I'.*

It is not that the world does not exist. As an appearance in consciousness, the world is the totality of the known in the potential of the unknown. *The world can be said to appear, but not be.* Duration of the appearances, of course, will differ according to the different scales of time. Apart from the fact that the world disappears in deep sleep and re-appears in the waking state, the duration of its appearance would vary according to the allotted span of one's life time — a few hours for an insect and aeons for the trinity of Brahmā, Vishnū and Maheshwara! Ultimately, however, whatever is an appearance in consciousness must end, and it cannot have any reality.

The manner in which Maharaj expounds this sublime knowledge is truly astonishing in its range of aspects while the central theme continues to remain firmly anchored. He says that awareness comes from the Absolute (Avyakta) and pervades the inner self (Vyakta). The outer self (Vyakti) is that part of one's being of which one is not aware, inasmuch as, although one may be conscious (for every sentient being has consciousness), it is possible for one not to be aware. In other words, the outer self (Vyakti) is delineated by the physical body; the inner self (Vyakta) by consciousness, and it is only in Pure Awareness that the Supreme (Avyakta) can be contacted.

There can never be any 'experience' as such of the Absolute for the simple reason that there cannot possibly be anything objective about the Absolute, which is essentially pure subjectivity. It is the inner self-consciousness which is the experiencing medium for all experience. The Absolute provides the potentiality for the experience; the self provides the actuality.

The individual person's contact with the awareness of the Absolute can come about only when the mind is 'fasting' as it were, because then the process of conceptualizing ceases. When the mind is quiet, it reflects Reality; when the mind is absolutely motionless it dissolves and only Reality remains. That is why, says Maharaj again and again, it is necessary to be one with consciousness. *When the mind feasts, Reality disappears; when the mind fasts, Reality enters.*

Awareness, Maharaj points out in yet another way, when it is in contact with an object, a physical form, becomes witnessing. When at the same time there is self-identification with the object, such a state becomes 'the person'. In Reality, there is only one state; when corrupted and tainted by self-identification, it may be called a person (Vyakti); when it is tinted by a sense of being, the resulting consciousness becomes 'the witnessing'; when it remains in its pristine purity, untainted and untinted, it is the Supreme, the Absolute.

It is necessary to be clear about the difference, notional though it be, between awareness of the Absolute and the consciousness in which the universe appears, Maharaj repeatedly warns us. One is only the reflection of the other. But reflection of the sun in the dew-drop is not the sun. In the absence of objectivization, as in deep sleep, the apparent universe is not, but we are. This is so, because what we are is what the apparent universe is, and *vice versa* — dual in presence, non-dual in absence; irreconcilably separate in concept, inviolably united when unconceived.   ●●

5

Awareness and Consciousness

The outstanding feature about Maharaj's talks with the visitors is the pervading sense of their total spontaneity. Subjects are never selected earlier, but Maharaj's utterances have a unique resilience which gives them an exhilarating freshness every time. And one marvels all the more when one recalls that he has been talking like this, without any previous preparation, two sessions a day, every day in the week including Sundays, for the last many years. And then, on top of this, Maharaj says with a chuckle of amusement: What do I talk about? Only one subject, the same subject — you and I, the world outside, and God.

Generally, Maharaj does not bother to wait for his audience before opening any topic that comes up in his mind. Sometimes his small loft-room gets filled to capacity within fifteen minutes or so. At other times, when he starts talking — one might say thinking aloud — there are hardly three or four persons present. But it makes no difference to him. He may talk even to a single seeker, if he so chooses, and expound to him with zest the basics of his teaching, relating them to each other and placing them in true perspective. His mind is whole mind that goes beyond pragmatism. His thinking is total thinking.

One morning, when I had paid my respects to Maharaj and sat down, I found that there were only two other persons present. Maharaj suddenly said: What is the difference between 'awareness' and 'consciousness', if any? When something like this happens, one does not really know whether he expects an answer, or whether he is merely thinking aloud. One hesitates to answer for fear of breaking the flow of his thoughts. But then, he might also say: Why don't you answer? Have you been wasting my time, listening to the talks all these days? This morning, however, he carried on without waiting for an answer.

He observed that awareness is of the Absolute, and, therefore, beyond the three Guṇas (Guṇātīta); whereas consciousness is something fed by, and limited by, the food-body. When the food-body is destroyed, consciousness also disappears. Mind you, no one dies — the body, made of the five elements mingles with the elements when it is lifeless, and consciousness, which is subject to the three Gunas, becomes free of the Gunas. Awareness is the primordial original state, prior to the concept of space-time, needing no cause, no support. It simply *is*. However, the moment the concept of consciousness arises on this original state of unicity, the sense 'I am' arises, causing a condition of duality. Consciousness is with a form, a reflection of awareness against the surface of matter. One cannot think of consciousness apart from awareness; there cannot be a reflection of the sun without the sun. But there can be awareness without consciousness. In deep sleep, for instance, there is no consciousness (it is resting) but awareness is certainly there, because, on waking, one is aware of having slept; but only on waking.

Maharaj never allows us to forget that it is consciousness alone which is our constant companion, and that it is the continuous attention to one's stream of consciousness that takes one on to Awareness — the basic existence, that-which-is-life-love-joy. According to Maharaj, the very consciousness of being conscious is already a movement towards Awareness. The mind by its very nature is out-going, always tending to seek the source of things within the things themselves. When it is directed towards the source within, it is almost like the beginning of a new life. Awareness replaces consciousness. The 'I am', which is a thought in consciousness, ceases. In awareness, there is no thought. Awareness is the source of consciousness. Maharaj suggests that it is an excellent spiritual exercise to sit quietly and watch what comes to the surface of the mind. What we call thoughts are like ripples on the surface of water. Thoughts always lead to identification or condemnation; they are products of pre-conceived notions and stand in the way of real understanding. Just as water is serene when free of ripples, so is the mind serene when free of thoughts, when it is passive and fully receptive.

In the mirror of your mind, says Maharaj, all kinds of pictures will appear, stay for a while and disappear. Silently watch them come and go. Be alert, but not attracted or repelled. It is important not to be involved. This attitude of silent witnessing will have the effect, gradually, of driving away all useless thoughts, like unwanted guests that are ignored. By being thus within yourself, that is, in the 'I-am-ness', by watching the flow of mind, without interfering or judging, as a dispassionate witness, the 'deep' unknown will be encouraged to come to the surface of consciousness and release its unused energies to enable you to understand the mystery of the origin of life.   ••

6

Bondage of Space and Time

Visitor: I remember reading somewhere that it is the combination of space and time which is the cause of one's bondage. I have since been wondering how possibly space and time could result in bondage.

Maharaj: Let us be clear what we are talking about. What do you mean by 'bondage', and bondage for whom? If you are satisfied with this world which you consider as real, and the way it has been treating you, where is the bondage for you?

V: Let me acknowledge that to me the world seems real enough, but it is not a fact that I am satisfied with my role in it. I feel deeply convinced that there must be very much more to life than just going through it, as most of us do — without any definite aim, merely routinely. From this point of view I think life itself is bondage.

M: When you use the word 'I' what exact image do you have about yourself? When you were a child you considered yourself nothing other than a child and were happy enough to play with toys. Later, you were a young man, with strength enough in your arms to tackle a couple of elephants, and you thought you could face anything or anyone in this world. You are now in your middle age, a little mellower but nonetheless enjoying life and its pleasures, and you think you are a happy and successful man, blessed with a nice family. At present you have an image about yourself that is quite different from the images you had earlier. Imagine yourself ten years hence and further twenty years later. The image you will then have about yourself will be different from all the earlier ones. Which one of these images is the real 'you'? Have you ever thought about it? Is there any particular identity that you can call your very own and which has remained with you throughout, unchanged and unchangeable?

V: Now that you mention it, I admit that when I use the word 'I', I have no particular idea about myself and I agree that whatever idea I have had about myself has been changing over the years.

M: Well, there *is* something which has remained unchanged all these years, while everything else has been changing. And that is the constant sense of *presence*, the sense that you *exist*. This sense or feeling 'I am', has never changed. This is your constant image. You are sitting in front of me. You know it beyond doubt, without any need of confirmation from anyone else. Similarly you know that you *are*, that you *exist*. Tell me, in the absence of what would you be unable to sense your existence?

V: If I were asleep or unconscious I would not know that I exist.

M: Exactly. Let us proceed further. In the morning, the very first moment when you wake up and your consciousness just takes over, do you not feel your conscious presence, your existence, 'I am', not as an individual person, but presence as such?

V: Yes, that is right. I would say that my individual personality comes into existence when I see my body and other objects around.

M: When you say that you see an object, what really happens is that your senses have reacted to a stimulus from an outside source, which is, external to your body apparatus. And what your senses have perceived and your mind has interpreted, is nothing but an appearance in your consciousness. This appearance in consciousness is construed as an event, extended in space and duration. All manifestation depends on a combination of the two closely knit media called space and time. In other words, in the absence of the space-time combination, no manifestation could possibly arise in consciousness. Are you following me?

V: Yes, I understand what you said. But where do I come in, as an individual, in this process?

M: This is exactly where the rub lies. All 'existence' is a continuous process of objectifying. We only exist as one another's objects and, as such, only in the consciousness that cognizes us. When objectivization ceases, as in deep sleep, the objective universe disappears.

So long as one imagines oneself as a separate entity, a person, one cannot see the total picture of the impersonal reality. And the idea of a separate personality is due to the illusion of space and time, which by themselves have no

independent existence for they are only instruments, mere
media to make manifestation cognizable.

At any time, only one thought or feeling or perception can
be reflected in consciousness, but thoughts feelings and
perceptions move on in succession giving the illusion of
duration. And personality comes into being simply because
of memory — identifying the present with the past and
projecting it into the future.

*Think of yourself as momentary, without a past or future,
then where is the personality?* Try this and find out for
yourself. In memory and anticipation, that is in the past and
the future, there is a clear feeling that there is a mental state
under observation, whereas in the actual the feeling is
primarily of being awake and present — here and now.

V: I think I understand. I must sit quietly and try to absorb
this wholly new way of thinking.

M: Now do you see how space and time, which come along
with consciousness and make manifestation perceivable, are
the culprits? All you can truly say is: 'I am' (meaning *what is,
is*). The moment there is a thought of 'me' as a separate
personality, there is what is termed 'bondage'. To realize
this is the end of all seeking. When you apperceive that
whatever you think yourself to be is only based on memory
and anticipation, your search ends and you stand aloof in full
awareness of the false as false.   ●●

7

How a Jnānī Sees the World

A lady visitor, taking advantage of the fact that it was the last day of her visit to Bombay, sought Maharaj's permission to ask what she called a 'silly' question.

Maharaj: All thoughts, all desires, holy or unholy, come from the self. They all depend upon the desire to be happy and, therefore, are based on the sense 'I am'. Their quality will depend on one's psyche (Antahkarana) and on the degrees at which the three Guṇas prevail. Tamas produces restraint and perversions; Rajas produces energy and passions; and Sattva produces harmony and the urge to make others happy. Now, what is your question?

Visitor: All these days — which have unfortunately flown away all too quickly — whilst you were talking, and your words were emerging as if by themselves without any preparation behind them, I have been wondering how you look at the objects which your eyes see, including the persons who are sitting before you. As today is the last day of my present visit, I thought I would venture to ask this rather silly question.

M: What makes you think that I see you as objects at all? You assume that it is with a certain special significance that I see things, a significance which escapes you. But that is not really your question. Your question essentially seems to be: How are things perceived by a Jnānī who sees as seeing should be done?

Please remember, *objects are really the perceiving of them*. Conversely, therefore, the perceiving of them is what the objects are. Try to understand.

When an object is seen as an object, there would have to be
a subject other than the object. As the Jnānī perceives, there
is neither the subject that sees nor the object that is seen;
only the 'seeing'. In other words, the Jnānī's perception is
prior to any interpretation by the sensory faculties. Even if
the normal process of objectification has taken place, the
Jnānī, in his perspective, has taken note of this fact and seen
the false as false. The Jnānī in his undivided vision, has
perceived that physically both the seer and the seen are
objects, and that the functioning of consciousness itself
merely produces effects in consciousness. Both the
producing and the perceiving are done by consciousness, in
consciousness. Try to understand this.

In short, the Jnānī's seeing is the whole-seeing, or
in-seeing, or intuitive seeing, seeing without any objective
quality — and that is freedom from bondage. That is what I
mean when I say: "I see, but I do not see."

And this is the silly answer to your silly question.   ●●

8

The Proof of Truth

Can there be proof of truth? Maharaj sometimes puts this
question, as if to himself. Can truth be grasped
intellectually?

Apart from keen intellect, says Maharaj, the seeker must
have faith to enable him to grasp the basic essentials of truth.

And the faith should be of the kind that can accept the Gurū's word as God's own truth. Faith is the first step, and no further progress is possible unless the first step is taken first.

There are simple-minded people, who, though not gifted with keen intellect, have abundant faith. Maharaj gives them a Mantra and asks them to chant it and meditate till their psyche is purified enough to receive knowledge.

With the intellectuals Maharaj has to deal differently. The intellectual understands what the various religions propagate, the ethical and moral codes they prescribe, also the metaphysical concepts they adumbrate; but he remains unenlightened. What he actually seeks is truth, the constant factor that is not subject to any change. And, what is more, he wants proof, but is not able to say what kind of proof would satisfy him. Proof as such would itself be something subject to space and time, and the intellectual is intelligent enough to know that. Truth, in order to be truth, must be timeless and spaceless. Maharaj says that any intelligent person must admit that 'I am', the sense of conscious presence, of 'being', is the only truth every sentient being knows of, and that is the only 'proof' one can have. And yet, mere existence can not be equated with truth for the simple reason that existence itself is not timeless and spaceless, like Reality.

Maharaj in his talks throws abundant light on this stalemate. A blind man may say: Prove to me that there are colours, only then will I believe all your lovely description of the rainbow. Whenever such questions are put to Maharaj, he counters them by saying: Prove to me that there is something like Bombay, or London, or New York! Everywhere, says he, it is the same earth, air, water, fire and sky. In other words, one cannot seek truth as an object, nor can truth be described. It can only be suggested or indicated, but not expressed in words, because truth cannot be conceived. Anything conceived will be an object and truth is not an object. As Maharaj puts it: You cannot 'shop' for truth, as something which is authoritatively certified and stamped as 'Truth'. Any attempt to find the proof of truth would involve a division of the mind into subject and object, and then the answer could not be the truth, because there is nothing objective about truth, which essentially is pure subjectivity.

The whole process, says Maharaj, is like a dog chasing its own tail. In seeking a solution to this riddle one must analyze the problem itself. Who is it that wants the proof of Truth or Reality? Do we clearly understand what we are? All existence is objective. We all 'exist' as objects only, as mere appearances in the consciousness that cognizes us. Is there really any proof that 'we' (who seek proof of Reality) ourselves exist, other than as objects of cognition in someone else's mind?

When we seek the proof of truth, what we are trying to do is equivalent to a shadow seeking proof of the substance! Maharaj, therefore, urges us to see the false as false, and then there will be no more looking for truth. Have you understood what I mean? he asks. Do you not *intuitively* feel what the position is? *That which is sought is the seeker himself!* Can an eye see itself? Please understand, he says: Timeless, spaceless, not cognizable sensorially is what we *are;* temporal, finite and sensorially cognizable, is what we *appear to be* as separate objects. Consider what you were before you acquired the physical form. Did you need any proof about anything then? The question of proof arises only in relative existence, and any proof provided within the parameters of relative existence can only be an untruth!••

9

You are Rāma, I am Rāma

Different types of people come to Maharaj with different motives. Usually he asks a new visitor to tell him something about himself — his family background, his business or profession, length of the period he has been interested in spiritual quest, the kind of Sādhanā, he has done and the specific reasons for his visit. Maharaj's intention, obviously, is to find out in what way and by what approach he could help each visitor personally, and, at the same time, ensure that the dialogue would also enlighten the other visitors.

Most of the visitors state briefly the required facts about themselves, and many of them say they had read his book *I Am That* and had ever since desired to sit at his feet and listen to him. In such cases, Maharaj would smile and nod his head. If anyone wanted to ask specific questions, Maharaj would ask him to sit closer so that the dialogue could be carried on more easily. Those who had no questions would be expected to sit further back.

Once when the session was about to begin two middleaged gentlemen walked in, paid their respects to Maharaj, and sat down. One of them told Maharaj that he was a senior Government Official and that he had no particular interest in spiritual matters. He had come there only to introduce his brother who was deeply interested. After introducing his companion as his brother the gentleman left.

Then the brother took over and told Maharaj that he had had a Gurū for many years but that he had passed away. He had received from the Gurū a Nāma Mantra and was told that its repetition, as often as possible, was the best Sādhanā, and he was following his Gurū's instructions. He said that he had now reached a stage where he believed that everything was Rāma and Rāma was in everything, and that he had attained through this Sādhanā a peace and joy not possible to be described in words. All this was stated by him in a manner as if he was making a great revelation for the benefit of the audience before him, including Maharaj himself. After this narration he looked round to see what effect it had created on the listeners. Then, with a complacent self-satisfaction he sat, eyes closed and smiling to himself.

Maharaj, serene and silent to all appearances, but with a sparkling glint in his eyes that the regular callers knew well, asked this visitor politely if he could be of help to him in any way. In answer, the gentleman, waving his right arm in a gesture of resignation, said that he did not want anything from anybody and that he had come to see Maharaj only because several people had pressed him to attend at least one session of his talks — and here he was!

Maharaj then asked the visitor if there was any specific purpose of his Sādhanā and what did he hope to achieve from it, if anything?

Visitor: When I sit in meditation, I often get lovely visions of my beloved Lord Rāma, and I am engulfed in bliss.

Maharaj: And when you are not in meditation?

V: I think of the Lord and see him in everyone and everything. (Maharaj listened to the answer with an expression of amusement and again there was the familiar glint in his eyes. We the regular visitors knew what was coming, for the glint often precedes Maharaj's verbal sally he sometimes makes to deflate hollow presumptions and destroy illusions. His lips formed into a question)

M: And what do you mean by 'Rāma'?

V: I don't understand the question. Rāma is Rāma.

M: When you see Rāma in me, Rāma in a dog and Rāma in a flower, what exactly do you mean by Rāma? And how exactly do you see Rāma? In his traditional pose with a string-bow on his shoulder, and arrows in his quiver?

V: (Rather confused) Yes, I think so.

M: And the peace and joy that you feel, when you sit in meditation and get visions of Rāma, would it be something like the peace and joy one would feel when, after a long and tiring walk in the scorching sun, one is able to rest under the shade of a spreading tree, enjoy the breeze that is blowing and drink some cool water?

V: You cannot really compare the two, because one is physical and the other is, I would say, mental or psychic.

M: In any case, would your Sādhanā enable you to have a clear understanding of your true nature?

V: What is the use of such a discussion? Rāma is God and I am only a poor human who has surrendered himself to Rāma.

M: Surrender is a very good and effective Sādhanā by itself. But we must very clearly understand what 'surrender' really means, though that is a separate subject by itself. Are you aware that Rāma, though a prince by birth, was only an ordinary human being like you, who did not become a god until he was duly initiated and instructed in knowledge by the sage Vasishtha? And what was the teaching which Vasishtha imparted to the young Rāma? Was it not Ātma-Jnāna, the knowledge of the self, the knowledge of one's true nature?

I would suggest that you throw away all the illusory concepts you have collected over the years, and begin with your own self. Think along these lines: What is my true nature? What is the 'capital' I am born with, and which has remained — faithful and unchanged — with me from the moment I had the knowledge that I exist? How did I acquire this body-construct along with the Prāna (the vital force) and the consciousness which gives me the sense of presence? How long will all this last? What was 'I' before this body came into being, and what will 'I' be after this body disintegrates? Who was really 'born' and who will 'die'? What am 'I'? It was such knowledge which turned Rāma from a human being into a god.

By this time, the visitor had realized that something was very much wanting in the Sādhanā, as he had practised it, without ever giving serious thought to the ultimate aim of his spiritual quest. He gave up his pretentious pose of being an enlightened person, and very humbly requested Maharaj for permission to visit him again during the few days he would be staying in Bombay. Maharaj lovingly told him that the sincerity and keenness of his desire to visit him was all the permission that was necessary. ••

10

Images in Imagination

Whatever be the subject of discussion at a session, Maharaj seems to see to it that the catechism follows the correct line of argument. And whenever somebody puts an irrelevant question Maharaj firmly but gently rules it out and brings the discussion back to the original theme.

Occasionally, however, Maharaj has to leave the room briefly on some errand, and during one such short interval, some one started talking about a politician who had prominently figured in the press that morning. He said that he knew the individual personally and that he was a conceited bully. Someone else immediately contradicted the speaker, saying that the man in question was a perfect gentleman and it was a calumny to speak ill of him. An argument between these two was about to start when Maharaj returned and they kept quiet.

Maharaj, however, sensed the sudden silence and asked what was going on. When he was told about the

contradictory opinions he was vastly amused. He sat still for
a few moments and then started talking. Why this difference
in the two opinions? he asked. Because the opinion-forming
was done through an individual viewpoint and not through
integral perception. Both the images of the same person
arose in the imagination of the viewers, both were entirely
their own mental creations and basically unrelated to the
object i.e. the person whose images these were supposed to
be. Creation of such images, said Maharaj, is due to the
functioning of dualistic discrimination — the 'me' and the
'other one'. This is indeed what may be called the original
sin; *this duality — the 'me' and the 'other' — is bondage.*
And if there is anything like liberation (in essence there is no
individual that is bound), it is indeed liberation from this
concept of 'me' and the 'other'. What is necessary, said
Maharaj, is to cease making snap conceptual judgements of
things as objects, and to turn one's attention back to the
subjective source. He asked us to 'reverse' our attention, to
go back to the infant state, even to think of what we were
before this body-mind complex was born, so that we would
stop conceptualizing about others all the time and getting
involved in mere mental images.

At this stage a visitor said: "Yes, Maharaj, I can clearly see
what you mean. But how can one get away from this
continuous conceptualizing which seems to be the very
warp and woof of one's conscious life?" Maharaj fixed his
gaze on the questioner and, almost before the Marathi
translation of his question had been completed, he
remarked: "Rubbish! You could not have understood my
point at all; if you had, your question could not arise."

He then proceeded to explain the process of
objectification. Whatever your senses perceive and your
mind interprets is an appearance in consciousness, extended
in space-time and objectivized in a world which, the
cognizing object (i.e. you) considers as separate from
himself. And this is where the whole error lies: in this
process perception is not total. What is necessary is *whole
seeing,* seeing not with the individual mind, which is a
divided mind, but seeing from within, seeing from the

source — seeing not from manifestation as a phenomenon but from the source of all seeing. Then, and only then, will there be total perception and correct seeing and apprehending.

Maharaj concluded by saying that what he had said was vitally important and needed (Manana) pondering and meditating over it, not mere verbal discussion.   ●●

11

The Play Goes On

Surprising though it may seem, Maharaj is a superb actor. His features are mobile and he has large, expressive eyes. When narrating an incident or discussing some subject, his features spontaneously respond to his words and actions. His speech is very articulate and when he talks he makes free use of gestures. It is, therefore, one thing to listen to a tape-recording of his talks and quite another to hear his vibrant voice accompanied by appropriate gesticulations. He is a star performer indeed.

One morning, among the listeners was a well-known European actor. Maharaj was explaining how the image one has about oneself is not a faithful one; it keeps on changing from time to time according to the changing circumstances. He went through the entire gamut of the usual life span, describing the image one has of oneself as an infant, sucking a nipple and wanting nothing else; then as a teenager bursting with health and strength and with ambitions to conquer the world; then a love-lorn man, followed by the weary bread-earner with family responsibilities, and finally on to a sick old man, hardly able to open his mouth and even incapable of controlling his bodily functions. Which is the real you? Which of these different images? he asked.

Maharaj's narration was alive with actions and sound effects appropriate to the various stages of life he described. It was sheer drama! We heard him in dumb admiration and the professional actor was flabbergasted. "Never before have I seen sucn a brilliant performance", said he, though he did not understand a word of the language that Maharaj spoke so effectively. He was simply spell-bound. While the actor marvelled, Maharaj, with a mischievous glint in his eyes, said to him: "I am a good actor. Am I not?" He added: Do you really understand what I am driving at, though? I know you have appreciated this little performance of mine. But what you have seen now is not even an infinitesimal part of what I am capable of doing. The whole universe is my stage. I not only act but I construct the stage and the equipment; I write the script and direct the actors. Yes, I am the one actor acting the roles of millions of people — and, what is more, this show never ends! The script is being continuously written, new roles are being conceived, new settings are propped up for many different situations. Am I not a wonderful actor/director/producer?

The truth however is, he added, that every one of you can say the same thing about himself. But, it is ironic indeed that once you are really able to feel with deep conviction that that is so, the show is over for you! Can you perceive that it is only you that is acting the role of every character in the world? Or, will you confine yourself to the limited one-bit role that you have assigned to yourself and live and die in that petty role?   ••

12

Manifestation is a Dream

Numerous casual visitors come to visit Maharaj just for a Darshan, perhaps because someone in their group spoke highly of him and, having nothing better to do, they thought they might as well drop in and see what the whole thing was about. But there are many who are deeply interested in the one subject about which Maharaj talks. Quite a few of them have attended several sessions and they honestly believe that they have a firm grasp of what Maharaj so earnestly talks about. Perhaps in answer to a query from Maharaj, if they have understood what he has been trying to convey, one of them would say: "Oh yes, Maharaj, I have clearly understood it. But, I have only one last question. . . . . . ."

The last question often happens to concern manifestation of the noumenon as phenomena. The questioner might say: Maharaj, you have said that the Absolute-noumenon is unaware of its awareness until consciousness begins to stir and the first thought 'I am' arises; and then the wholeness is broken up into duality and manifestation of the universe takes place. My question is: Why did the first thought arise and why manifestation took place at all?

Maharaj would look at the questioner with an expression indicating several reactions. A mixture of compassion, appreciation of the questioner's sincerity, a certain amount of amusement at the confidence with which he thinks he has understood the subject, but — most important — a disappointment that the questioner had not understood the point after all. Another failure!

Maharaj would than say, very softly: I am afraid you have not really grasped what you have been hearing. You have been hearing, but not listening. You have been hearing what I have been saying, as a collection of little bits and pieces, not listening to the whole; hearing words with the divided mind of the individual instead of listening to the meaning with the whole mind; hearing as a separate hearer, not listening after integrating yourself with the Guru. And I do not mean the physical, individual Guru which you would have in mind but the Sadguru within yourself. Otherwise, this question would not have arisen. But, in a way, I myself am rather fond of such enquiry because it exposes the usual way of thinking; or rather, the thinking exposes itself.

Consider, to whom did this question occur? Where did it occur? Did the question not occur to a 'you' who considers himself an entity with an independent existence? And did it not occur in consciousness? There would be no entity — this supposed pseudo-entity — in the absence of consciousness, and 'consciousness' is only a concept without any objective quality whatsoever, and as such without any phenomenal existence.

What we have arrived at, then, is this: In the absence of the substratum of consciousness there is no manifestation, and, therefore, no separate pseudo-entities to ask any questions at all! And consciousness is only a concept. Therefore, I call the entire manifestation 'the child of a barren woman.' In these circumstances, can this-which-is, this-that-we-are, ever be understood by the tainted mind of a conceptual pseudo-entity? Indeed, it is only when this entity disappears that the mystery dissolves, for the simple reason that *the searcher is what he is searching for!*

Your question, moreover, assumes that basically manifestation and non-manifestation are two different 'things' but they are not. They are essentially the same state, like waves on an expanse of water. When coloured by a sense of *being*, it is consciousness in which manifestation appears with its limitations; when colourless and limitless, it is the Absolute, unaware of its awareness. The phenomena are only the *mirroring* of the noumenon; they are not different. Noumenon is like (again a concept in order to make communication possible) the one source of electricity passing through a number of 'exhibits' such as lamps, fans, motors etc., or like the one source of light reflected in myriad of mirrors — consciousness manifesting itself through millions of sentient forms.

Now, do you see your question in the correct perspective? A shadow wants to know 'why'? One of the characters played by a single actor taking various roles in a one-man play wants to know why? The answer could well be: Why not? Actually there could not be any question — neither why nor why not — because there really is no questioner at all, only a concept. Manifestation is like dream. Why does a dream occur? ●●

13

Love and God

The dialogue, one evening, was started by a young Canadian, wearing a Lungi and a thin Kurta. He said he was twenty-three, but looked barely out of his teens. He wore around his neck an elegant little silver cross on a dainty chain. He said he had come across the book *I Am That* in a bookshop in Bombay a couple of days ago. A cursory glance at a few pages impelled in him a desire to meet Maharaj personally. He had already gone through the book reading almost continuously, through the afternoon, evening and night, and had finished both the volumes only a few hours ago.

Maharaj: You are so young. I wonder since what age you

have been interested in the spiritual quest.

Visitor: Sir, ever since I remember I have been deeply interested in Love and God. And I strongly felt that they are not different. When I sit in meditation, I often . . . .

M: Wait a moment. What exactly do you mean by meditation?

V: I don't really know. All I do is to sit cross-legged, close my eyes, and remain absolutely quiet. I find my body relaxing, almost melting away, and my mind, or being or whatever merging into space, and the thought-process getting gradually suspended.

M: That's good. Please proceed.

V: Quite often, during meditation, an overwhelming feeling of ecstatic love arises in my heart together with an effusion of well-being. I do not know what it is. It is during one such spell that I felt inspired to visit India — and here I am.

M: How long will you be in Bombay?

V: I really don't know. I rarely make any plans. I have sufficient money to live frugally for about fifteen days, and I have my return ticket.

M: Now tell me, what is it exactly that you want to know. Do you have any specific questions?

V: I was a very confused man when I landed in Bombay. I felt I was almost going out of my mind. I really don't know what took me to the bookshop because I don't do much reading. The moment I picked up the first volume of *I Am That*, I experienced the same overpowering feeling that I get during my meditation. As I went on reading the book a weight seemed to lift off from within me, and, as I am sitting here before you, I feel as if I am talking to myself. And what I am saying to myself seems like blasphemy. I was convinced that love is God. But now I think that love is surely a concept and if love is a concept God also must be a concept.

M: So, what is wrong in it?

V: (Laughing) Now, if you put it like that I have no feeling of guilt in transforming God into a concept.

M: Actually, you said love is God. What do you mean by the word 'love'. Do you mean 'love' as the opposite of 'hate'? Or, do you mean something else, although, of course, no word can be adequate to describe 'God'.

V: No. No. By the word 'love' I certainly do not mean the opposite of 'hate'. What I mean is that love is abstaining from discrimination as 'me' and the 'other'.

M: In other words, unity of being?

V: Yes, indeed. What then is 'God' to whom I am expected to pray?

M: Let us talk about prayer later. Now then, what exactly is this 'God' you are talking about? Is he not the very consciousness — the sense of 'being' that one has — because of which you are able to ask questions? *'I am' itself is God.* What is it that you love most? Is it not this 'I am', the conscious presence which you want to preserve at any cost? The seeking itself is God. In seeking you discover that 'you' are apart from this body-mind complex. If you were not conscious, would the world exist for you? Would there be any idea of a God? And, the consciousness in you and the consciousness in me — are they different? Are they not separate only as concepts, seeking unity unconceived, and is that not love?

V: Now, I understand what is meant by 'God is nearer to me than I am to myself'.

M: Also remember, *there can be no proof of Reality other than being it.* Indeed you *are* it, and have always been. Consciousness leaves with the end of the body (and is therefore time-bound) and with it leaves the duality which is the basis of consciousness and manifestation.

V: What then is prayer, and what is its purpose?

M: Prayer, as it is generally understood, is nothing but begging for something. Actually, prayer means communion-uniting-Yoga.

V: Everything is so clear now, as if a great deal of rubbish has been suddenly thrown out of my system, blown out of existence.

M: Do you mean that you now seem to see everything clearly?

V: No. No! Not 'seems'. It *is* clear, so clear that I am now amazed that it was not clear at any time. Various statements that I had read in the Bible, which seemed important but vague before, are now crystal clear — statements like: Before Abraham was I am; I and my father are one; I am that I am.

M: Good. Now that you know what it is all about, what Sādhanā will you do to obtain liberation from your 'bondage'?

V: Ah! Maharaj. Now you are surely making fun of me. Or, are you testing me? Surely, now I know and have realized that *I am that — I am, which I have always been and which I shall always be*. What is left to be done? Or, undone? And who is to do it? And for what purpose?

M: Excellent! *Just be.*

V: I shall, indeed.

Then, the young Canadian prostrated before Maharaj, his eyes brimming with tears of gratitude and joy. Maharaj asked him if he would be coming again, and the lad said: "Honestly, I don't know." When he left, Maharaj sat for a while with his eyes closed, the gentlest of smiles on his lips. He then said very softly: "A rare one"; I could barely catch the words.

I never saw the young Canadian again, and I have often wondered about him.   ●●

14

Standpoint for Reading the Gītā

At one of the sessions a distinguished-looking lady visitor wanted to ask a question about the **Bhagavadgītā**. While she was framing her question in proper words, Maharaj suddenly asked her: "From what standpoint do you read the Gītā?"

Visitor: From the standpoint that the Gītā is perhaps the most important guide for the spiritual seeker.

Maharaj: Why do you give such a stupid answer? Of course it is a very important guide for the spiritual seeker; it is not a book of fiction. My question is: What is the standpoint from which you read the book?

Another visitor: Sir, I read it as one of the Arjunas in the world for whose benefit the Lord was gracious enough to expound the Gītā. When Maharaj looked around for other answers there was only a general murmur in confirmation of this answer.

M: Why not read the Gītā from the standpoint of Lord Krishna? To this suggestion there were simultaneously two types of startled reactions from two of the visitors. One was a shocked exclamation which clearly meant that the suggestion would tantamount to a sacrilege. The other was one single crisp clap of hands, a reflex action obviously denoting something like Archimedes' *eureka*. Both the concerned visitors were rather embarrassed by their unwitting articulation and by the fact that the two reactions were the exact opposite of each other. Maharaj gave the clapper' a quick look of approval and continued:

M: Most religious books are supposed to be the spoken word of some enlightened person. However enlightened a person, he must speak on the basis of certain concepts that he finds acceptable. But the remarkable distinction of the Gītā is that Lord Krishna has spoken from the standpoint that he is the source of all manifestation, i.e. from the standpoint not of the phenomenon, but of the noumenon, from the standpoint 'the total manifestation is myself'. This is the uniqueness of the Gītā.

Now, said Maharaj, consider what must have happened before any ancient religious text got recorded. In every case, the enlightened person must have had thoughts which he must have put into words, and the words used may not have been quite adequate to convey his exact thoughts. The master's words would have been heard by the person who recorded them, and what he recorded would surely have been according to his own understanding and interpretation. After this first handwritten record, various copies of it would have been made by several persons and the copies could have contained numerous errors. In other words, what the reader at any particular time reads and tries to assimilate could be quite different from what was really intended to be conveyed by the original master. Add to all this the unwitting or deliberate interpolations by various scholars in the course of centuries, and you will understand the problem I am trying to convey to you.

I am told that the Buddha himself spoke only in the Māghadī language, whilst his teaching, as recorded, is in Pālī or in Sanskrit, which could have been done only many many years later; and what we now have of his teaching must have passed through numerous hands. Imagine the number of alterations and additions that must have crept into it over a long period. Is it then any wonder that now there are differences of opinion and disputes about what the Buddha actually did say, or intended to say?

In these circumstances, when I ask you to read the Gītā from the standpoint of Lord Krishna, I ask you to give up at once the identity with the body-mind complex when reading it. I ask you to read it from the point of view that you are the animating consciousness — the Krishna-consciousness — and not the phenomenal object to which it gives sentience — so that the knowledge that is the Gītā may be truly unfolded to you. You will then understand that in the Vishva-rūpa-darshan what Lord Krishna showed Arjuna was not only his own Svarūpa, but the Svarūpa — the true identity —of Arjuna himself, and thus, of all the readers of the Gītā.

In short, read the Gītā from the standpoint of Lord Krishna, as the Krishna-consciousness; you will then realize that a phenomenon can not be 'liberated' because it has no independent existence; it is only an illusion, a shadow. If the Gītā is read in this spirit, the consciousness, which has mistakenly identified itself with the body-mind construct, will become aware of its true nature and merge with its source.   ••

15

Blind Youth with True Vision

Once, at the end of a rather long dialogue-cum-discourse session, during which Maharaj repeatedly brought his listeners to the basic point of his teaching (that the conscious presence, 'I am', is the original concept on which everything else appears, and that this concept itself is only an illusion) he asked the question: Have you understood what I am trying to say?

This question was addressed to the listeners generally. All were silent, but one among them said: "Yes Maharaj, I have understood your words intellectually, but...." Maharaj heard the answer and smiled wearily, perhaps because he was amused by the fact that the speaker, though he said he understood, had not really understood. He then proceeded further to explain the subject lucidly in a categorical manner as follows:

1. The knowledge *I am* or consciousness is the only 'capital' a sentient being has. Indeed, without consciousness he would not have any sentience.

2. When this *I-am-ness* is not present, as in deep sleep, there is no body, no outside world, and no 'God'. It is evident that a tiny speck of this consciousness contains the entire universe.

3. Nevertheless, consciousness cannot exist without a physical body, and existence of the body being temporal, consciousness also must be temporal.

4. Finally, if consciousness is time-bound and is not eternal, any knowledge that is acquired through the medium of consciousness cannot be the truth and is, therefore, ultimately to be rejected, or, as I said, to be offered to Brahman as an oblation — Brahman being consciousness, beingness, I-am-ness, or Ishwara, or God, or whatever name you give it. In other words, the inter-related opposites, both knowledge and ignorance, are in the area of the known and, therefore, not the truth — and truth is only in the unknown. Once this is clearly understood, nothing more remains to be done. Indeed there is really no 'entity' to do anything.

After uttering these words Maharaj became silent and closed his eyes. The little loft-room seemed to be submerged into an effulgent peace. Not a word was spoken by anybody. Why is it, I wondered, that most of us are unable to see and

feel the dynamic manifestation of truth presented by
Maharaj time and again. And why some of us — though very
few — see it in a flash.

After some time, when Maharaj opened his eyes and we all
reverted to the normal state, someone drew his attention to
the poor, blind young man who had recently attended his
talks only twice, in the morning and again the same evening,
and had gone back 'liberated'. At the end of the session,
when this young man bade goodbye to Maharaj, he was
asked whether he had understood what it was all about and
he had said confidently: "Yes". When Maharaj himself asked
him what he had understood, he sat quietly for a few
moments, and then spoke: Maharaj, I do not have the right
words to express my feelings of gratitude to you for making
the whole picture so very clear to me, so simply, and so
quickly. I can summarize your teaching:

1. You asked me to remember what I *was* before I had this
   knowledge 'I am' together with the body, i.e., before I
   was 'born';
2. You told me that this body-cum-consciousness had come
   upon me without my knowledge or concurrence,
   therefore 'I' had never been 'born';
3. This body-cum-consciousness that is 'born' is
   time-bound and, when it disappears at the end of its
   allotted span, I shall be back in my original state, which is
   always present, but not in manifestation;
4. Therefore, I am not consciousness, and certainly not the
   physical construct which houses this consciousness;
5. Finally, I understand that there is only 'I' — neither 'me',
   nor 'mine', nor 'you' — only *that which is*. There is no
   bondage other than the concept of a separate 'me' and
   'mine' in this totality of manifestation and functioning.

After hearing these words from the blind youth, uttered
with absolute conviction, Maharaj had given him a look of
understanding and love, and had asked him: "Now what will
you be doing?" The answer was: "Sir, I have understood you
truly. I will be doing nothing. 'Living' will go on." He then
paid his respects to Maharaj with great adoration and left.

The blind young man was not really blind, said Maharaj.
He had the true vision. There are few like him.   ••

16

He Came to Scoff . . .

When one participates in the dialogues between Maharaj
and his visitors over a period, one is astonished at the range
of questions that are asked — many of them shockingly naive
— and the spontaneity and ease with which the answers
come from Maharaj. Both the questions and answers are
translated as accurately as possible. Maharaj's answers in
Marathi, which is the only language he is fluent in, would
naturally be based on the Marathi words used in the
translation of the question. In his answers, however,
Maharaj makes very clever use of the Marathi words used in
the translation of the question, either by way of puns or by a
slight change in the words themselves, producing
interpretations sometimes totally different from their usual
meaning. The exact significance of such words could never
be brought out in any translations. Maharaj frankly admits
that it is usually in the lighter vein that he uses the Marathi
language in exposing the mental level of the questioner and
the intent and the conditioning behind his question. If the
questioner treats the session as an entertainment, albeit of a
superior kind, Maharaj is ready to join in the fun in the
absence of better subjects and better company!

Among the visitors, there is occasionally an unusual type

of person who has a very keen intellect but is armed with a devastating skepticism. He is cock-sure that he has an open mind and a penetrating intellectual curiosity. He wants to be convinced and not merely cajoled by vague and woolly words that religious teachers often dole out in their discourses. Maharaj, of course, is quick to recognize this type and then the conversation at once assumes a piquancy that leaves one stunned. The intuitive perception underlying the words of Maharaj simply sweeps away the metaphysical quibbles put forward by such an intellectual. One wonders how a man who did not have even the benefit of proper schooling can prove more than a match for pedantic scholars and skeptical agnostics who believe themselves to be invulnerable. Maharaj's words are always galvanic and scintillating. He never quotes authorities from the scriptures in Sanskrit or any other language. If one of the visitors should quote even a fairly familiar verse from the Gītā, Maharaj has to ask for a Marathi translation of it. His intuitive perception needs no support by way of the words from any other authority. His own internal resources are limitless indeed. Whatever I say, says Maharaj, stands by itself, it needs no support.

One of the usual visitors at the session had brought with him a friend and introduced him to Maharaj as a man with a very keen intellect who would not take anything for granted and who would question everything before accepting it. Maharaj said he was happy to meet such a person. The new visitor was a professor of mathematics.

Maharaj suggested that it would perhaps be best for the two of them to have a dialogue without assumptions of any kind; right from the basic level. Would he like that? The visitor must have been most pleasantly surprized at this offer. He said he was delighted at the suggestion.

Maharaj: Now, tell me, you are sitting before me here and now. What exactly do you think 'you' are?

Visitor: I am a male human being, forty-nine years old, with certain physical measurements and with certain hopes and aspirations.

M: What was your image about yourself ten years ago? Same as it is now? And when you were ten years old? And when you were an infant? And, even before that? Has not your image about yourself changed all the time?

V: Yes, what I considered as my identity has been changing all the time.

M: And yet, is there not something, when you think about yourself — deep down — that has not changed?

V: Yes, there is, though I cannot specify what exactly it is.

M: Is it not the simple sense of *being*, the sense of existing, the sense of *presence*? If you were not conscious, would your body *exist* for you? Would there be any world for you? Would there then be any question of God or the Creator?

V: This is certainly something to ponder. But tell me, please, how do you see yourself?

M: I am *this-I-am* or, if you prefer, I am *that-I-am*.

V: I am sorry, but I don't understand.

M: When you say "I think I understand", it is all wrong. When you say "I don't understand", that is absolutely true. Let me make it simpler: I am the conscious presence — not this individual or that, but *Conscious Presence, as such.*

V: Now, again I was about to say, I think I understand! But you have just said that that is wrong. You are not deliberately trying to get me confused, are you?

M: On the contrary, I am telling you the exact position. Objectively, *I am all* that appears in the mirror of consciousness. Absolutely, *I am that. I am the consciousness in which the world appears.*

V: I am afraid, I don't see that. All I can see is what appears before me.

M: Would you be able to see what appears before you if you were not conscious? No. Is all existence, therefore, not purely objective inasmuch as you exist only in my consciousness, and I in yours? Is it not clear that our experience of one another is limited to an act of cognition in consciousness? In other words, what we call our existence is merely in the mind of some one else and, therefore, only conceptual? Ponder over this too.

V: Are you trying to tell me that we are all mere phenomena in consciousness, phantoms in the world? And what about the world itself? And all the events that occur?

M: Ponder over what I have said. Can you find a flaw in it? The physical body, which one generally identifies with oneself, is only the physical construct for the Prāna (the life-force) and consciousness. Without the Prāna-consciousness what is the physical body? Only a cadaver! It is only because consciousness has mistakenly identified itself with its physical covering — the psychosomatic apparatus — that the individual comes into existence.

V: Now, you and I are separate individuals who have to live and work in this world along with millions of others, of course. How do you view me?

M: I view you in this world exactly as you view yourself in your dream. Does that satisfy you? In a dream whilst your body is resting in your bed, you have created a whole world — parallel to what you call the 'real' world — in which there are people, including yourself. How do you view yourself in your dream? In the waking state, the world emerges and you are taken into what I would call a waking-dream state. While you are dreaming, your dream-world appears to you very real indeed, does it not? How do you know that this world that you call 'real' is also not a dream? It is a dream from which you must awaken yourself by seeing the false as false, the unreal as unreal, the transient as transient; it can 'exist' only in conceptual space-time. And then, after such an 'awakening' you are in Reality. Then you see the world as 'living', as a phenomenal dream within the periphery of sensorial perception in space-time with a supposed volitional freedom.

Now, about what you call an individual: Why don't you examine this phenomenon analytically, of course with an open mind, after giving up all existing mental conditioning and preconceived ideas? If you do so, what will you find?

The body is merely a physical construct for the life-force (Prāṇa) and consciousness, which constitute a sort of psychosomatic apparatus; and this 'individual' does nothing other than responding to outside stimuli and producing illusory images and interpretations. And, further, this individual sentient being can 'exist' only as an object in the consciousness that cognizes it! It is just an hallucination.

V: Do you really mean to say that you see no difference between a dream dreamt by me and my living in this world?

M: You have had quite a lot already to cogitate and meditate upon. Are you sure you wish me to proceed?

V: I am used to large doses of serious study, and I have no doubt you too are. I would be most grateful indeed if we could proceed further and take this to its logical conclusion.

M: Very well. When you were in deep sleep, did the phenomenal world exist for you? Can you not intuitively and naturally visualize your pristine state — your original *being* — before this body-consciousness condition intruded upon you unasked, unaided? In that state, were you conscious of your 'existence'? Certainly not.

The universal manifestation is only in consciousness, but the 'awakened' one has his centre of seeing in the Absolute. In the original state of pure *being*, not aware of its *beingness*, consciousness arises like a wave on an expanse of water, and in consciousness the world appears and disappears. The waves rise and fall, but the expanse of water remains. *Before all beginnings, after all endings, I am. Whatever happens, 'I' must be there to witness it.*

It is not that the world does not 'exist'. Exist it does, but merely as an appearance in consciousness — the totality of the known manifested, in the infinity of the unknown, unmanifested. *What begins must end. What appears must disappear.* The duration of appearance is a matter of relativity, but the principle is that whatever is subject to time and duration must end, and is, therefore, not real.

Now, can you not apperceive that in this living-dream you are still asleep, that all that is cognizable is contained in this phantasy of living; and that the one, who whilst cognizing this objectified world considers oneself an 'entity' apart from the totality which is cognized, is actually very much an integral part of the very hypothetical world?

Also, consider: We seem to be convinced that we live a life of our own, according to our own wishes and hopes and ambitions, according to our own plan and design through our own individual efforts. But is that really so? Or, are we being dreamed and lived without volition, totally as puppets, exactly as in a personal dream? Think! Never forget that just as the world exists, albeit as an appearance, the dreamed figures too, in either dream, must have a content — they are what the dream-subject is. That is why I say: *Relatively 'I' am not, but the manifested universe is myself.*

V: I think I am beginning to get the whole idea.

M: Is not thinking itself a notion in the mind? Thought is absent in seeing things intuitively. When you think you understand, you don't. When you perceive directly, there is no thinking. *You know that you are alive; you do not 'think' that you are alive.*

V: Good heavens! This seems to be a new dimension that you are presenting.

M: Well, I don't know about a new dimension, but you have expressed it well. It could indeed be said to be a fresh direction of measurement — a new centre of vision — inasmuch as by avoiding thought and perceiving things directly, conceptualizing is avoided. In other words, in seeing with the whole mind, intuitively, the apparent seer disappears, and the seeing becomes the seen.

The visitor then got up, paid his respects to Maharaj with considerably more devotion and submission than was shown by him on his arrival. He looked into Maharaj's eyes and smiled. When Maharaj asked him why he was smiling, he said he was reminded of a saying in English: 'They came to scoff, and remained to pray!'   ••

17

Noumenon and Phenomena

It was one of those mornings, perhaps a Monday, when there were only a few of us, the regular 'addicts'. Maharaj sat with his eyes closed, still like a statue. After some time he suddenly started speaking softly, so softly that we unconsciously moved nearer to him. He continued to sit with his eyes closed, and went on speaking, or rather thinking aloud: People think that I am a Jnānī. They come to me from all over the world — from Canada to Australia and New Zealand, from England to Japan. Most of them have read *I Am That* and come all the way to Bombay only to meet me. With great difficulty they are able to locate this little old house of mine in a dirty, narrow street. They climb up the stairs and find a small dark man in the simplest of clothing, sitting in a corner. They think: This man doesn't look like a Jnānī; he does not dress impressively, as someone known as Nisargadatta Maharaj could be expected to do. Could he really be the one?

What can I say to these people? I tell them quite frankly that my education is up to the level which can barely put me in the category of the literate; I have not read any of the great traditional scriptures and the only language I know is my native Marathi. The. only enquiry I have pursued, but pursued it relentlessly — like a hunter pursues his quarry — is this: 'I know *I am* and I have a body. How could this happen without my knowledge and consent? And what is this knowledge *I am?*' This has been my life-long pursuit and I am fully satisfied with the answers I have reached. This is my only Jnāna, yet people believe I am a Jnānī. My Gurū told me: "You *are* Brahman, you are all and everything.

There is nothing other than you." I accepted my Gurū's word as truth, and now, for forty odd years I have been sitting in this very room doing nothing except talking about it. Why do people come to me from distant lands? What a miracle!

After pursuing my enquiry to its logical conclusion what have I arrived at? The whole thing is really simple, if only one sees the picture clearly. What is this 'me' that I am concerned with? The immediate answer, of course, is — 'this me, this body'. But then the body is only a psychosomatic apparatus. What is the most important element in this apparatus which qualifies it to be known as a sentient being? It is undoubtedly the consciousness without which this apparatus, while perhaps technically alive, would be useless as far its functioning is concerned. This consciousness obviously needs a physical construct in which to manifest itself. So, consciousness depends upon the body. But what is the body made of? How does the body come into existence? The body is merely a growth in the woman's womb during a period of about nine months, the growth of what is conceived by the union of the male and female sexual fluids. These fluids are the essence of the food consumed by the parents. Basically, therefore, both consciousness and the body are made of, and are sustained by food. Indeed, the body itself is food — one body being the food of some other body. When the food-essence, the vital sexual fluids, grows from conception into a tiny body and is delivered out of the mother's womb, it is called 'birth'. And when this food essence gets decayed due to age or illness and the psychosomatic apparatus happens to get destroyed, it is called 'death'. This is what happens all the time — the objective universe projecting and dissolving innumerable forms; the picture keeps on changing all the time. But how am 'I' concerned with this? I am merely the witness to all this happening. Whatever happens during the period of the happening, in each case, affects only the psychosomatic apparatus, not the 'I' that I am.

This is the extent of my 'knowledge', basically. Once it is clear that whatever happens in the manifested world is something apart from me, as *the 'I'*, all other questions resolve themselves.

At what stage exactly did I come to have the knowledge of my 'existence'? What was I before this knowledge 'I am' came to me? This knowledge 'I am' has been with me ever since I can remember, perhaps a few months after this body was born. Therefore, memory itself must have come with this knowledge 'I am', this consciousness. What was the position before that? The answer is: *I do not know.* Therefore, whatever I know of anything has its beginning in consciousness, including pain and pleasure, day and night, waking and sleeping — indeed the entire gamut of dualities and opposites in which one cannot exist without the other. Again, what was the position before consciousness arose? These interrelated opposites inevitably must have existed but only in negation, in unicity, in wholeness. This must then be the answer. This unicity is what *I am*. But this unicity, this identity, this wholeness cannot know itself because in it there exists no subject as separate from an object — a position that is necessary for the process of seeing, or knowing, or cognizing. In other words, in the original state of unicity, or wholeness, no medium or instrument exists through which 'knowing' may take place.

Mind cannot be used to transcend the mind. The eye cannot see itself; taste cannot taste itself; sound cannot hear itself. 'Phenomena' cannot be phenomena without 'noumenon'. The limit of possible conceptualization — the abstract of mind — is noumenon, the infinity of the unknown. Noumenon, the only subject, objectifies itself and perceives the universe, manifesting phenomenally within itself, but apparently outside, in order to be a perceivable object. For the noumenon to manifest itself objectively as the phenomenal universe, the concept of space-time comes into operation because objects, in order to be cognizable, have to be extended in space by giving them volume and must be stretched in duration or time because otherwise they could not be perceived.

So, now I have the whole picture: The sentient being is

only a very small part within the process of the apparent mirrorization of the noumenon into the phenomenal universe. It is only one object in the total objectivization and, as such, 'we' can have no nature of our own. And yet — and this is important— phenomena are not something separately created, or even projected, but are indeed noumenon conceptualized or objectivized. In other words, the difference is purely notional. Without the notion, they are ever inseparable, and there is no real duality between noumenon and phenomena.

This identity — this inseparableness — is the key to the understanding, or rather the apperceiving of our true nature, because if this basic unity between the noumenon and the phenomenon is lost sight of, we would get bogged down in the quagmire of objectivization and concepts. Once it is understood that the *noumenon is all that we are*, and that *the phenomena are what we appear to be as separate objects*, it will also be understood that no entity can be involved in what we *are*, and therefore, the concept of an entity needing 'liberation' will be seen as nonsense; and 'liberation', if any, will be seen as liberation from the very concept of bondage and liberation.

When I think about what I was before I was 'born', I know that this concept of 'I am' was not there. In the absence of consciousness, there is no conceptualizing; and whatever seeing takes place is not what one — an entity — sees as a subject/object, but is seeing from within, from the source of all seeing. And then, through this 'awakening', I realize that the all-enveloping wholeness of the Absolute can not have even a touch of the relative imperfection; and so I must, relatively, live through the allotted span of life until at the end of it, this relative 'knowledge' merges in the no-knowing state of the Absolute. This temporary condition of 'I-know' and 'I-know-that-I-know' then merges into that eternal state of 'I-do-not-know' and 'I-do-not-know' that 'I-do-not-know.   ●●

18

Let us Understand Basic Facts

Almost all the visitors from abroad come to Maharaj after having read his book *I Am That*. They say that on reading it, they felt a compulsive desire to meet Maharaj personally. Quite a few of them also say that they had been interested in the spiritual quest for many years.

Let us take the case of an average foreign visitor. His first visit almost invariably raises a certain amount of doubt in his mind, whether he had done the right thing in spending so much money and his hard-earned annual leave in coming here. The dirty surroundings of Maharaj's house, the simplicity of his tiny loft-room, his unimpressive physical appearance and his plain attire — all these contribute to the initial doubt. Of course, after attending a couple of sessions and, certainly by the time he leaves, the foreign visitor, is already looking forward to his next visit!

There is also one other factor which initially keeps pricking the foreign visitor's mind. Maharaj's behaviour is not unlike that of any other common man on the street. And it goes against his concept of how a sage, or Jnānī, should behave, though this concept itself may be exceedingly vague. He finds the walls of Maharaj's small room cluttered with pictures of numerous gods and saints. He sees him participating in the chanting of Bhajans four times a day. He finds him smoking cheap country-made cigarettes all the time, and sometimes talking on trivial matters in a light-hearted manner. He finds all this very confusing. His pre-conceived notion about Maharaj was perhaps that of a saffron-robed patriarchal figure, conversing gravely from an elevated seat some distance away from the visitors, occasionally bringing about a miracle or two in a condescending manner. Instead, he finds an utterly ordinary man!

It is, therefore, not surprizing that before the end of the very first session, our visitor cannot resist the temptation of asking why Maharaj, inspite of being a Jnānī, sings Bhajans four times a day. Or, perhaps, the question could be: Why does Maharaj find it necessary to smoke? Maharaj's usual answer in such cases is simple: Why not? I have been associated with this body for eighty-odd years; why should it not receive the few crumbs which it has got used to? As for Bhajans four times a day, it is a practice from the times of my Gurū. If since then I have had what is usually called 'awakening', should I feel compelled to give up this old and harmless routine? One must go through one's allotted span of time. Does it matter what one does, so long as one does not knowingly hurt any one else? It is as simple as that.

Maharaj continues with this theme somewhat as under: If one sees — apperceives — things as they are, if one apprehends the total manifestation with the whole mind and not with the dichotomized mind of an individual, one is not far away from the great awakening, and then whatever one does is of no importance. Indeed, to think that an individual being can act independently is itself a mistake. What we are is the conscious presence, and not the outside casing of consciousness; not the body which is only a psychosomatic apparatus used for cognizing the manifestation. This apparatus is only a spacio-temporal concept and as such has no independent existence and, therefore, cannot act independently, despite all appearances to the contrary. Let us understand this basic fact.

What then is life? Life in this universe is nothing other than the 'functioning of manifestation', despite what each individual might think. Viewed in this perspective, the various destructive manifestations like floods and earthquakes lose their sting. Each body is nothing but food for some one else — mouse for a cat, man or beast for a lion, lamb or

chicken for man and so on. So what is good for one is evil for
another; indeed whatever events seem to happen constitute
nothing but the functioning of manifestation. To each individual it all appears to be his own doing and experiencing,
but the fundamental fact is that no phenomenal object (and
that is all that a sentient being, relatively, is) can have any
independent existence of its own. Once this is clearly apprehended, it will automatically follow that all responsibility and guilt are also imaginary concepts, based upon the
mistaken notion that a sentient being has independent existence, autonomy and choice of action.

Then, what about all the eminent examplars in the various
spheres of human activity — the arts, sciences, atheletics —
the greatest thinkers? We must admire the work done by
consciousness 'through' these various physical forms, but
not the individual persons who are nothing more than conceptual phenomena. Let us understand and be clear about
what really happens. The question that would follow is: If
the individual persons do not achieve whatever has been
achieved, who does? The answer is: No one individually.
The 'functioning' of the manifestation takes place in consciousness through Prajñā. that brilliant actor/producer of
this total dream-show, who assumes all the roles in the great
dream-drama that this manifestation is. And the source of
this conscious presence is the noumenon. Sentient beings
appear to act and react, but the real functioning happens in
consciousness.

Let us, says Maharaj, admire the azure sky, the lovely
moon and the twinkling stars; let us write poems about the
beauty of nature; let us love the many Avatāras that have
descended upon the earth through the ages, let us sing Bhajans four times a day but, let us at least understand the true
position! *I, noumenon, am all the 'functioning' in
consciousness!*

Finally, we may ask ourselves: What then are we doing all
day? Are we not living our lives, we the millions of people in
the world? If we could think deeply and rationally about
what we know as life, we would easily come to the conclu-

sion that all that we do, throughout the day and day after day, is nothing but objectifying. Indeed, manifestation is itself nothing but continuous objectivization, because, when in deep sleep consciousness rests objectivization necessarily ceases; so does the objectified universe. In deep sleep, there is no self, no world, no God.

What we think as 'doing' is nothing but objectivization; functioning of manifestation takes place so long as there is consciousness. By unnecessarily identifying oneself as the doer one attracts responsibility and guilt. When the mind, which is the content of consciousness, is blank — when it 'fasts' or rests — the spinning and weaving of the mind ceases, and it calms down. *When the mind stops 'doing', it merely is.* In the absence of objectivization, our absolute presence *is*, the manifested universe *is not* — we *are*. Or, rather, '*I am*'. Let us at least understand these basic facts. ••

19

Self-knowledge and Problems of Life

One morning, the session was enlivened by the visit of a well-known social and political figure, a retired Indian diplomat, whose presence generally makes for a good-humoured and lively discussion. This morning the subject was whether self-knowledge and the practical life in the world could go together. Were they complementary, or were they contrary to each other.

This visitor is not only not unfamiliar with Maharaj's teaching but has imbibed it sincerely, though it would seem that once in a while his basic proclivities towards social and political catharsis would give him a feeling of spiritual instability, underlining the need for a quick refresher course. Apart from this, he loves Maharaj greatly and does not mind driving down the distance of about 100 miles to Bombay only to see him.

His basic question was: Can a man honestly afford to spend his time absorbed in meditation on the self, to the exclusion of the many social and political problems in the country and the world?

The most refreshing part of Maharaj's talks is his unique approach to problems referred to him. He says that we should forget the conceptual jungle that grows quickly around any theme as well as the directives of the traditional scriptures and should get down to the fundamentals. Maharaj tackled the question of this distinguished visitor with his customary *elan*.

Let us deal with the matter, he said — you and I — now. There have been numerous great personalities and Avatāras in the world during the past two to three thousand years. Each one of them had laid down his own list of 'do's and 'don't's, depending on his own concept of the right and wrong and the needs of the times as he saw them. So far so good. Let us now also ask ourselves: What have all these great men and Avatāras achieved? Have they been able to make the slightest change in the behaviour of man or nature? There must be some reason — some fundamental reason — why they had not been successful. Could it be that the problem itself had been misconceived, or misperceived? Could it be that attacking the problem directly was like attacking the heads of a Hydra which when cut off are replaced instantly by others? And that the only way to decimate the Hydra was to locate its heart and strike there?

Now, said Maharaj, what are the basic ingredients of any

social, political, economic or any other problem? When we reduce the problem to its basic essentials, what do we find? The essentials are: I, you· (representing the millions of people) and the physical world. On analyzing these basic essentials what do we find? *All me's and you's and the earth, the sky, the moon and the stars — are they not mere conceptual images in consciousness?* All existence is objective. All me's and you's exist as one another's objects in the consciousness that cognizes them. And so far as the 'world', or 'universe' is concerned, is it in essence any different from the world which you create in your dream (or, more accurately, the world that *gets created* in your dream-consciousness) and which is made of the same ingredients and inhabited by the same kind of people, including yourself, as in what you call the 'real' world? Your 'real' world, you might say, had been existing long before you were born. Well, in your dream-world also there are seas and mountains and buildings and people which have obviously been existing for a long, long time. Are you going to solve the many social and political problems of the people in your personal dream?

Is it not therefore true, continued Maharaj, that the heart of the Hydra — the root of the problem — is consciousness in which the entire manifested universe appears? Indeed, is not consciousness the Hydra itself! And is it not consciousness on which the entire attention should be directed? Its nature, the cause of its appearance, and other relevant factors? Since it is consciousness in which the entire phenomenal world appears, it necessarily follows that all manifestation will become sensorially perceptible only if it is extended spacially and for a certain duration of time. One must, therefore, necessarily accept the purely conceptual existence of the psychic apparatus of space-time as a prerequisite for the perception of the manifested universe.

This leads us to the following conclusions:
1. Without the concept of space-time the manifested universe would not be sensorially perceptible; and,

therefore, all events based on cause and effect and
extended in space-time must also be only conceptual;

2. If the manifested universe is only an appearance (in the
absence of consciousness the universe cannot exist on its
own) then the manifested universe is the reflection of
something that is present in its own right;

3. Phenomena, then, are the objective aspect of the
noumenon, the total potentiality — the totality of the
known in the infinity of the unknown. Consciousness
cannot be used to transcend consciousness, and,
therefore, noumenon represents the outside parameter of
cognition;

4. Noumenon — *that-which-is* — can only *be*, and it can *be*
only now. In the absence of the conceptual space-time,
there can be absolutely no 'where', or 'when' for any
'thing' to *be*. Now that we see that the 'world' (problems
wherein are to be solved) is only an appearance, let us get
back to the me's and you's, who are supposed to solve the
world's problems. Before we start to identify the world's
problems and proceed to solve them, should we not
identify ourselves?

We are, relatively, sentient beings and we want to 'do'
something to solve the problems in the world. Is it possible
for a sentient being, who is itself conceptual, to do anything
that is other than conceptual? What do we do from morning
through night (except during deep sleep) other than
continuously objectivizing? And is the human body, which
is actually nothing but a psychosomatic apparatus, capable of
'doing' anything other than producing illusory images and
interpretations? Whatever we may think of ourselves (and
this image keeps on changing from time to time and there is
nothing stable about it) 'we' cannot but be an integral part of
the total manifestation and the total functioning, and cannot
in any manner be apart from it. We are better able to
comprehend this in the case of a personal dream which we
can review after waking up. What appears as oneself in the
dream, with an independent identity, is clearly seen (on a
review after waking) to be totally devoid of any independent

substance, a mere puppet being manipulated. Is it really any different in the world that we think of as 'real'? Ponder over this. Could it not be that we dream that we are awake, we dream that we are asleep, and all the time life is being lived; all a product of the dreaming mind — objectivization going on in consciousness. And what is consciousness itself but only a concept which comes like an eclipse on the noumenon for a certain length of time?

If this position is perceived directly, intuitively, then we know that in relativity *we are the conscious presence,* the animating consciousness and not the phenomenal object to which it gives sentience. When we see the false as false, the problem resolves itself. *We are the content of this living-dream,* actors in this living-drama. And actors can only play their roles, nothing more.

The distinguished visitor heard Maharaj in baffled silence. He had no words to express what he thought or felt.   ••

20

Gurū's Grace is All I Need

To the usual query from Maharaj, the visitor from Calcutta gave the relevant information about himself. He said that he had been interested in self-knowledge for the past many years. He had met almost every well-known saint in the northern India and many others not so well-known (Maharaj smiled when this was translated to him). He added that he had studied all the principal Upanishads, various commentaries on the Gitā in English and Bengali by different scholars. He was quite well-versed in the Sanskrit language also and had studied most of the traditional scriptures in the original. He felt that all he needed now was the Gurū's grace. He also said that he had read *I Am That* and was so deeply impressed with it that he had selected Maharaj as his final Gurū and he would not leave Bombay without receiving his grace. Also, that there was a time limit within which Maharaj must bestow that grace because his leave would expire on a particular date and he had already booked his return ticket for Calcutta on a certain day! By now Maharaj could not restrain a very broad smile.

Maharaj: I would like to ask you something.

Visitor: Yes sir. (He pushed out his chest and spoke with the confidence of a well-prepared candidate appearing for a *viva voce* examination.)

M: You have read many books and met many Jnānīs; so you must have by now found your own true identity. Tell me, what is your true identity as far as you yourself are concerned?

V: Sir, I am an humble seeker seeking enlightenment and

have come to you with the confident hope that you will not refuse me your grace.

M: You still have quite a few days here, so there is plenty of time for grace, or enlightenment! Let us first find out who it is that wants enlightenment. Indeed, let us find out whether there is any need at all for enlightenment or freedom, or Moksha, or whatever. Now let me have your answer to my question: Have you come to know your own true identity? Forget for the moment the world and the Gurū and God.

V: This is a very awkward question, sir. All I want is grace of the Gurū, without which the door will not open to me.

M: But should we not find out first whether there is at all a closed door barring your entry? Entry into what? You keep talking of the Gurū. What is your idea of a Gurū? You see, unless these basic questions are first answered to your own satisfaction, how can we proceed? Therefore, I repeat: After so many years of study, have you been able to find out your true indentity; this 'you' who is seeking the Gurū's grace in order to attain enlightenment?

V: Sir, I am sorry to say that you are making me very confused. All I can say in answer to your question is: I don't know.

M: Ah! now we are getting somewhere — "I don't know." No one has ever spoken words truer than these. Indeed that is the only truth and everything else is false.

V: Sir, I would have thought that you were making fun of me. But the look on your face suggests that you could hardly be more serious.

M: Now, please try to understand. You have done quite a bit of reading and you should be able to apprehend what I am saying. Try, and for a moment forget all that you have accumulated by way of knowledge, and grasp with an empty mind what I tell you — remember, an empty mind, empty, but keen; not just void and inert.

Whatever the state is when we did not know anything, that is our true state, that is Reality. In that state, we did not even know our own existence. Then, spontaneously, came the message or thought, or the knowledge 'I am'. This knowledge 'I am' started the sense of duality — subject and object, sin and merit and the entire gamut of inter-related opposites. *Whatever was before the knowledge 'I am' is truth; whatever is subsequent to the knowledge, or consciousness of 'I am', is false.* Understand this basic fact. I-am-ness, the sense of presence has been given various laudatory names like Māyā, Prakṛiti, Īshwara etc., but nevertheless it is an illusion, pure ignorance. It is Prakṛiti that, with the co-operation of conceptual Purusha (both constituting the parenthood principle) creates the world and peoples it with innumerable physical forms. It is Māyā in action that makes consciousness (which gives sentience to the sentient being) mistakenly believe that it is the particular form itself. Consciousness thus assumes the identity of the particular form, and forgets its true nature. Are you with me so far? Any questions?

V: Sir, I am following you single-mindedly. No questions.

M: Good. So far in this process, you will have noticed, there is no question of an 'entity' with independent existence. *You are that, which is prior to the arrival of I-am-ness.* What has come upon your true nature is like an illness, or an eclipse for a certain duration, at the end of which the physical form will 'die' and will be buried or cremated and will thereafter mingle with the five elements of which it was made. The life-force of breath will disappear and mingle with the air outside the body; consciousness will be freed of the limitation of the body and the three Gunas. In other words, the process will have reached its allotted end. Now, let us come back to your problem: Who is it that needs the Gurū's grace in order to attain 'liberation'? And liberation from which 'bondage'?

V: Maharaj, you have turned the problem around 180 degrees. You have reduced all my labour of forty years to zero and you have nullified my very existence. You have liquidated me! What can I say? The only thing is that in liquidating me you have also liquidated the Gurū!

M: Not quite, although that is not a bad reaction. Now listen further. The trouble is that you look upon yourself as an individual entity with a physical form; and you also look upon the Gurū as another individual entity with another form, albeit with something in his head or heart or somewhere, which makes him an 'enlightened' person but nevertheless a 'person' all the same. This is the real mistake. The Gurū however has realized that he is the Ultimate Reality; he sees every being as he sees himself, i.e. not as a 'person', nor as a mere 'form', or 'thing'.

The other mistake is that the seeker, the disciple, as an entity, expects to learn and understand 'something'. But how can a mere conceptual object understand anything? What actually happens is that *the understanding, as such, makes the seeker (the Sādhaka) disappear*. The individuality of the seeker gradually disappears, but, in the process, the Gurū's grace, which is always present like the shining sun, becomes one with consciousness. The sooner the identification with the body as a separate entity is lost the sooner will the Gurū's grace bloom in the consciousness of the disciple. And then he will realize that the Gurū is none other than the consciousness within, and it is consciousness which, pleased with the faith and love of the disciple, will act as the Sadgurū and unfold all the knowledge that is necessary. However, there cannot be any progress (though 'progress' itself is an erroneous concept) if you continue to regard yourself as an entity and expect the Gurū, as another entity, to give you some homework to do, and when that is duly completed, to award you a sort of certificate, or something, on a platter as 'liberation'. This whole concept is misconceived. You must realize the true significance of the Gurū and his grace before the ever-present Gurū's grace can smoothly and naturally flow towards you.

The visitor sat dumbfounded for a few moments. When he could find words, he said: "Sir, you have opened my eyes and made me see the falsity and futility of what I considered to be knowledge and Sādhanā. I have no words to express my gratefulness to you." He prostrated before Maharaj and left — an humbler and a wiser man.   ••

21

The Seed of Consciousness

He looked fidgety and agitated. His movements were jerky, and he was obviously bursting with impatience. This was a middleaged European, slim and physically very fit. It was his first visit to Maharaj. His restlessness drew everybody's attention to him.

As Maharaj looked at him tears suddenly welled up in his eyes. A compassionate glance from Maharaj seemed to compose him a little and he gave the usual preliminary information about himself in a few words. He said he had been a student of Vedānta for at least twenty years, but his search for truth had proved abortive. He was deeply despondent and disillusioned and he could not continue the frustrating pursuit any longer. A flash of hope had come to him when he read Maharaj's book *I Am That* and he knew that he had found the answer. Immediately he had got together the minimum amount of cash needed for the journey to India and he had just arrived in Bombay. In a choked voice he said "I have now arrived. My search is over." Tears were flowing freely from his eyes and he could hardly control himself.

Maharaj listened to him gravely and sat still for a few minutes with his eyes closed, perhaps to give him time to compose himself. Then he asked him whether he was firmly convinced that he was not the body. The visitor confirmed that it was quite clear to him that he was not merely the body but something other than the body, and, as was clearly explained in the book, that something must be the knowledge 'I am', the sense of being. But, he added, he could not understand what was meant by the suggestion that he should remain continuously with this knowledge 'I am'. What exactly was he supposed to do? "Please sir," he told Maharaj "I am now unbearably tired of words. I have read and heard them in millions and have not gained anything. Give me the substance now, not mere words. I shall be eternally grateful to you."

"Very well", said Maharaj, "You will have the substance now. Of course, I will have to use words to convey it to you." Maharaj then proceeded: If I say, *reverse and go back to the source of your beingness*, will it make any sense to you?

In reply, the visitor said that his heart intuitively accepted the truth of Maharaj's statement, but he would have to go deeper into the matter.

Maharaj then told him that he must understand the whole position clearly and instantly; this he could do only if he went to the root of the matter. He must find out how the knowledge 'I am' first appeared. The seed is the thing, said Maharaj. Find out the seed of this beingness, and you will know the seed of the entire universe.

Maharaj went on: As you know, you have the body and in the body is the Prāna, or the life-force, and consciousness (or the beingness, or the knowledge 'I am'). Now, this total phenomenon of the human being, is it any different from that of the other creatures, or even the grass which sprouts up from the earth? Think over it deeply. Suppose a little water accumulates in your backyard; after a time, the body of an insect forms itself there; it begins to move, and it knows that it exists. Then again, suppose a piece of stale bread is left in a corner for some days; a worm makes its appearance in it and begins to move, and it knows that it exists. The egg of a fowl, after being hatched for certain length of time, suddenly breaks open and a little chick appears; it begins to move about, and it knows that it exists. The sperm of man germinated in the womb of woman, after the nine-month period, is delivered as a baby. The sperm, developed into the form of a full-grown infant, goes through the states of sleeping and waking, carries out its usual physical functions, and knows that it exists.

In all these cases — the insect, the worm, the chicken and the human being — what is it that is really born? What is it that has 'supervised' the process from conception to delivery? Is it not the knowledge 'I am' that has remained latent from conception to delivery, and in due course, is 'born'? This beingness or consciousness, identical in all the four cases, finding itself without any kind of 'support', mistakenly identifies itself with the particular form it has assumed. In other words, what is really without any shape or form, the knowledge 'I am', just the sense of beingness (not being this, or being that, but consciousness generally), limits itself to only one particular form and thereby accepts its own 'birth', and thereafter lives in the constant shadow of the terror of 'death'. Thus is born the notion of an individual personality, or identity, or ego.

Now, do you see the source of I-am-ness? Is it not dependent on the body for its individual existence? And is not the body merely the germinated sperm which has developed itself? And, importantly, is the sperm anything other than the essence of the food consumed by the father of the child? And, finally, is not the food something thrown up by the four elements (ether, air, fire and water) through the medium of the fifth element, the earth?

The seed of consciousness is thus traced to nothing but food and the body is the 'food' of consciousness; as soon as the body dies consciousness also disappears. And yet, consciousness is the 'seed' of the entire universe! Every single individual, whenever he dreams, has identical experience of a world being created in consciousness. When a person is not quite awake and consciousness is just stirring, he dreams; and in his dream, in that minimal spot of consciousness, is created an entire dream-world, similar to the 'real' world outside — all in a split-second — and in that world are seen the sun, the earth, with hills and rivers, buildings, and people (including the dreamer himself), behaving exactly like the people in the 'real' world. Whilst the dream lasts, the dream-world is very real indeed, and the experiences of the people in the dream, including the dreamer himself, appear to be true, tangible and authentic.

perhaps even more so than those of the 'real' world. But once
the dreamer wakes up, the entire dream-world with all its
'realities' that then existed, collapses into the consciousness
in which it was created. In the waking state, the world
emerges because of the seed of ignorance (Māyā,
consciousness, beingness, Prakriti, Īshwara etc.) and takes
you into a waking-dream-state! Both sleep and waking are
conceptual states in the living-dream. *You dream that you
are awake; you dream that you are asleep — and you do not
realize that you are dreaming because you are still in the
dream.* Indeed, when you do realize that this is all a dream,
you will have already 'awakened'! Only the Jnani knows true
waking and true sleep.

At this stage, when the visitor was asked by Maharaj if he
had any questions on what he had heard so far, he promptly
asked: "What is the principle, or the conceptual mechanism
behind the creation of the world?"

Maharaj was pleased that the visitor had correctly used the
words 'conceptual mechanism', because he often reminds us
that the entire creation of the world is conceptual, and that it
is most important to remember this fact and not to forget it in
the midst of all the profusion of words and concepts. Maharaj
then continued: The original state — the Parabrahman — is
unconditioned, without attributes, without form, without
identity. Indeed, that state is nothing but fullness (not an
empty 'void', but plenum) so that it is impossible to give it
any adequate name. For the sake of communication,
however, a number of words have been used to 'indicate'
that state. In that original state, prior to any concept,
consciousness — the thought 'I am — spontaneously stirs
into existence. How? Why? For no apparent reason — like a
gentle wave on an expanse of water!

The thought 'I am' is the seed of the sound Aum, the
primordial sound or Nada at the start of the creation of
universe. It consists of three sounds: *a, u* and *m*. These three
sounds represent the three attributes — Sattva, Rajas,
Tamas, which have produced the three states of waking,
dreaming and deep sleep (also named consciousness or

harmony, activity and rest). It is in consciousness that the
world has emerged. Indeed, the very first thought 'I am' has
created the sense of duality in the original state of unicity.
No creation can take place without the duality of parenthood
principle — male and female, Purusha and Prakriti.

Creation of the world, as an appearance in consciousness,
has a ten-fold aspect — the parent principle of duality; the
physical and chemical material, being the essence of the five
elements (ether, air, fire, water and earth) under mutual
friction; and the three attributes of Sattva, Rajas and Tamas.
An individual may think that it is he who acts, but it is truly
the essence of the five elements, the Prana, the life-force,
which acts through the particular combination of the three
attributes in a particular physical form.

When creation of the world is viewed in this perspective,
it is easy to understand why the thoughts and actions of one
individual (which is actually nothing but a psychosomatic
apparatus) differ so much in quality and degree from those of
the millions of others. Why there are Mahatma Gandhis at
one end and Hitlers at the other. It is a well-established fact
that fingerprints of one person are never exactly similar to
those of any other person; leaves of the same tree are found
different from one another in minute details. The reason is
that the permutations and combinations of the five elements,
plus the three attributes in their millions of shades, would go
into billions and trillions. Let us by all means admire what
we think is admirable and love what we think is lovable, but
let us understand what it is that we really love and admire —
not the conceptual individual but the wonderful acting
ability of consciousness which is able to play simultaneously
millions of roles in this dream-play that the world is!

To avoid being lost in the bewildering diversity of the play
of Maya (Lila), said Maharaj, it is necessary at this stage not to
forget the essential unity between the Absolute and the
relative, between the non-manifest and the manifest
Manifestation comes into existence only with the basic
concept, 'I am'. The substratum is the noumenon, which is
total potentiality. With the arising of 'I-am-ness' it *mirrors*

itself into the pnenomenal universe which only appears to be exterior to the noumenon. In order to see itself, noumenon objectifies itself into phenomenon and for this objectivization to take place, space and time are the necessary concepts (in which the phenomena are extended in volume and duration). Phenomenon, therefore, is not something different from noumenon, but it is noumenon itself when objectivized. It is necessary to understand — and never to forget — this essential identity. Once the concept 'I am' arises, the fundamental unity gets notionally separated, as subject and object, in duality.

When impersonal consciousness manifests itself and identifies itself with each physical form the I-notion arises, and this I-notion, forgetting that it has no independent entity, converts its original subjectivity into an object with intentions, wants and desires, and is, therefore, vulnerable to suffering. This mistaken identity is precisely the 'bondage' from which liberation is to be sought.

And what is 'liberation'? Liberation, enlightenment, or awakening, is nothing other than understanding profoundly, *apperceiving* — (a) that the seed of all manifestation is the impersonal consciousness, (b) that what is being sought is the unmanifested aspect of manifestation and (c) that, therefore, the seeker himself is the sought!

Summarizing the discourse Maharaj said: Let us get it all together once again.

1. In the original state prevails *I am,* without any knowledge or conditioning, without attributes, without form or identity.

2. Then, for no apparent reason (other than that it is its nature to do so), arises the thought or concept *I am,* the Impersonal Consciousness, on which the world appears as a living-dream.

3. Consciousness, in order to manifest itself, needs a form, a physical body, with which it identifies itself and thus starts the concept of 'bondage', with an imaginary objectivization of 'I'. Whenever one thinks and acts from the standpoint of this self-identification, one could be

said to have committed the 'original sin' of turning pure subjectivity (the limitless potential) into an object, a limited actuality.

4. No object has an independent existence of its own, and, therefore, an object cannot awaken itself from the living-dream; yet — and this is the joke — the phantom individual (an object) seeks some other object, as the 'Absolute' or 'Reality' or whatever.

5. If this is clear, one must reverse and go back to find out what one originally was (and always has been) before consciousness arose.

6. At this stage comes the 'awakening' that one is neither the body nor even the consciousness, but the unnameable state of total potentiality, prior to the arrival of consciousness (in consciousness, that state, with whatever name, can only be a concept).

7. And so the circle is complete; *the seeker is the sought.*

In conclusion, said Maharaj, understand profoundly that, as 'I', one is noumenal. The current condition of phenomenonality (the seed of which is consciousness) is a temporary one, like a disease or an eclipse on one's original changeless condition of noumenality, and all that one can do is to go through one's allotted span of living, at the end of which the eclipse of phenomenality is over and noumenality prevails again in its pure unicity, totally unaware of its awareness.

Through all this exposition the visitor sat still, as if under a spell. He made an unsuccessful effort or two to talk, but Maharaj quickly stopped him with a firm gesture, and he sat there in perfect peace until after other visitors had paid their respects to Maharaj and left, one by one.   ••

22

Self-realization is
Effortless

It is the practice of Maharaj to expound a particular point in depth with great patience, giving apt examples and similies. After that when he asks for questions on what has been said, the queries often tend to be based not on the point which he has been at such pains to expound but on the examples which he had given merely to illustrate a particular aspect of the subject under discussion. Such questions clearly show that the questioners have missed the main point altogether. Maharaj, therefore, often exhorts the visitors: You may ask questions on what has been said but do so without identifying yourself with the body.

Many visitors feel rebuffed when the invitation to ask questions is thus made subject to a condition which appears to them rather onerous, even unfair. Why does Maharaj insist that the questioner should dis-identify himself from the body? The direct answer would be: Because an object cannot presume to understand its subject; it is impossible for a shadow to understand the substance of which it is a shadow.

So long as there is a conceptual 'individual' identifying himself with the body (which is merely a psychosomatic apparatus, an 'object') as an autonomous entity, can it be possible for him to understand anything at all about the Absolute, which is totally untouched by the objective? And further, can any queries from someone, thinking and speaking as a supposedly autonomous entity, be anything but arrant absurdity? It, however, does not imply that questions could arise only from a fully realized being. A realized being, a Jnānī, would have no questions at all!

What Maharaj would seem to expect of his listeners is something midway between these two extremes. As he often says, he assumes that those who come to him would not be just tyros but will have already done a fair amount of homework on the subject, not Mumukshūs but Sādhakas. In other words, Maharaj wants the listener not to forget that he is the impersonal consciousness, and not the physical apparatus in which consciousness has manifested itself. He expects that listening to him should be on the basis of direct apperceiving, without any intervention by the conceptual individual, and with a clear understanding of what is functioning during the process of talking and listening. In this context, Maharaj says: In order to be effective, the receptivity for my words must be such that they penetrate like an arrow. I speak to consciousness and not to any individual.

Maharaj's advice to listeners is 'to apperceive directly and forget immediately'; not to use his words as a platform from which to launch their own concepts. Concepts, he says, arise from thoughts, and all these together form a bundle that is known as mind. 'Thinking' means 'conceptualizing', creating objects in mind, and this is 'bondage'. Words, basically dualistic and conceptual, are an obstruction to enlightenment. They can only serve the temporary purpose of communication, but thereafter they are a bondage. Getting rid of conceptual thinking means enlightenment, awakening, which cannot be otherwise 'attained', or 'obtained' by any one. Enlightenment is not a 'thing', to be acquired by any one, at any time, at any place. Penetration of Maharaj's words like an arrow brings about this apperception and that is enlightenment!

To this the visitors' spontaneous reaction is: If there is no 'one' to acquire any 'thing', what are we expected to do? Maharaj's equally quick counter-question is: Who is 'we'? The answer usually comes — if it comes — tardily, hesitantly: You mean 'we' itself is part of the conceptual thinking? Totally illusory?

At this stage Maharaj repeats what he has always been saying: *All knowledge is conceptual, therefore, untrue*. Apperceive directly and give up the search for knowledge. But how many of you will do so? How many of you understand what I am trying to convey to you? What is the purpose of all my talks? asks Maharaj. It is to make you understand, to see, to apperceive your true nature. But first there is a hindrance to be removed; or rather, a hindrance that must disappear before you can see and *be* the *what-is*. All 'thinking', 'conceptualizing', 'objectivizing' must cease. Why? Because *what-is* does not have the slightest touch of objectivity. It is the subject of all objects, and not being an object it cannot be observed. The eye sees everything else, but cannot see itself.

To the question 'what does one have to do, what efforts must one make to stop conceptualizing', Maharaj's answer is: Nothing; no efforts. Who is to make the effort? What effort did you make to grow from a tiny sperm cell to a full grown baby in your mother's womb? And thereafter, for several months when you grew from the helpless baby to an infant, what efforts did you make to sense your presence? And now you talk of 'efforts', which 'you' must make! What efforts can an illusory, conceptual 'I' make to know its true nature? What efforts can a shadow make to know its substance? Realizing one's true nature requires no phenomenal effort. *Enlightenment cannot be attained, nor forced. It can only happen*, when it is given the opportunity to do so, when obstruction by concepts ceases. *It can appear only when it is given a vacant space to appear in*. If someone else is to occupy this house, says Maharaj, I must first vacate it. If the conceptual 'I' is already in occupation, how can enlightenment enter? Let the conceptual 'I' vacate and give enlightenment a chance to enter. Even making a positive effort to stop thinking as a method of getting rid of conceptualizing, is an exercise in futility, and so is any other kind of 'effort'!

The only effective effort is instant apperceiving of truth.

See the false as false and what remains is true. What is absent now will appear when what is now present disappears. It is as simple as that. Negation is the only answer.   ●●

23

Child of a Barren Woman

Maharaj is extremely alert to ensure that, in response to his invitation to ask questions, the visitors do not start a discussion amongst themselves and thus get entangled into an intricate web of their respective concepts, to the exclusion of the subject which he had been expounding. When there are signs of this happening, he is so very amused that he is wont to remark: "Ah, now we are discussing details of the wedding ceremony of the child of a barren woman!"

Maharaj uses this simile of 'the child of a barren woman' fairly frequently. One morning, a visitor, who had perhaps heard it for the first time, was quite intrigued and requested him to illustrate it by an example. For a while, Maharaj remained silent with his eyes closed, without the least movement, his breathing as shallow as could be, and we thought he would go into a Samādhi. But then he started talking in a low voice: Look, understand what time is. Unless you know the nature of time, you will not understand the nature of phenomena. What happens is that one takes time for granted and then proceeds to build all kinds of concepts.

If you are going to build, should you not first see what your foundation is like?

Time and space go together. Why are you able to cognize things? Because you see them. Would you have been able to see things if they had no form? You see things because they have form, volume, because they are extended into space. Let us go a step further: If things were seen in space for a split-second only, would you be able to perceive them? You perceive things, only because they are extended into space for a certain duration (time), and the forms remain long enough before you to enable you to perceive them.

If there were no concepts of time and space (time and space themselves are obviously not objects), 'things' would not be perceptible and things would not be 'things'. If there were no space-time (no past, present, and future), how could there have been any phenomena, any events? Please try to understand that both phenomena and time are merely concepts and have no existence of their own: Whatever things are seen, or thought of, are merely images conceived in consciousness, the supposed actuality of which is as 'real' as a dream or a mirage. Now do you understand what I mean when I say that all phenomenality is the child of a barren woman?

This point about space-time, said Maharaj, is so difficult to grasp that even highly intelligent people are baffled and confounded at its complexity and are unable to comprehend its true significance. At this stage he addressed a question to the visitors generally: "Have the scientists ever gone deeply into the problem of the nature of space-time?"

There were various comments, but the consensus was that no scientists had really made a deep study of this problem, but that some of the topmost among them, including Einstein, had come to the conclusion that the entire universe is 'of the nature of thought', and they held that the nature of space-time is really incomprehensible since it crosses the borders of the mind and all human knowledge acquired so far.

Maharaj laughed and said: How can the scientists do it

with their puny minds? They may conceive 'unlimited space' and 'unlimited time', but can they conceive the very *absence* of space and time? It is impossible because that which conceives, in its conception, cannot conceive the conceiving. Would it be possible for the eye to see its own seeing? Can the fire burn itself? Can water understand thirst?

If you can grasp the significance of what I have said, you will cease looking at 'things' against the fixed background of time; you will cease searching for truth through the medium of your proud intellect. Indeed, you will realize that the very effort of searching is an obstruction because the instrument with which you will be searching is a divided mind — a conceptual subject seeking a conceptual object. When you realize this, you will stop searching and let the impersonal consciousness take over. And then, when the impersonal consciousness lets you in on the mystery of its own source, *you will know that there is no 'you', or 'me', but only 'I'*, the essential subjectivity; that 'things' have no substance and, therefore, a phenomenon is the child of a barren woman; and, finally, that 'I' am intemporality, infinity!   ••

24

A Review of the Fundamentals

A foreign visitor who could spend only three days in Bombay attended both the morning and evening sessions every day. At the final session, he said that during the three days he had absorbed so much that he was not able to sort out the priorities and did not know what to do first and what could be postponed. He earnestly requested Maharaj to review the fundamentals so that he could retain them in his mind in an orderly manner.

Maharaj laughed and asked him if there was any confusion in his mind about his being a male human being, about being the son of his parents, or about his profession! If not, then why should there be any confusion about his true nature!

Anyway, said Maharaj, let us take up what you have asked for. What you really want is to reach an acceptable understanding of your self (which you have been conditioned to regard as a body-mind entity with complete control over its actions) and your relationship with the world in which you live — you on the one hand and the world on the other.

Now, what you think you are, is nothing but the 'material' essence of your father's body which was conceived in your mother's womb, and which later grew spontaneously into the shape of a baby with bones, flesh, blood etc. Indeed, you were not even consulted about your 'birth'. A human form was created which grew from a baby to an infant and at a certain time, perhaps in the second year of your life, you were told that 'you' were born, that 'you' have both a name

and a form. Thereafter, you had the knowledge of your
'beingness' and 'you' began to consider yourself as a
separate individual, with an independent entity, apart from
the rest of the world. Now consider: (i) Did your parents
specially and deliberately create 'you'? (ii) Did your parents
know the moment when conception took place? (iii) Did
'you' specifically and deliberately select a particular couple
as your parents? and (iv) Did you choose to get 'born'?

From the answers to these questions it would be clear that
a form in the shape of a human being got created almost
accidentally (without any concurrence or selection on any
one's part), which you subsequently accepted as your self.
Therefore, 'you' as such do not exist either as a 'fact', or as an
entity. This is the first fundamental. A form got created
through a natural process.

Then, the question is what are 'we' — all of us? Each one of
us, as a phenomenon, is merely an appearance in the
consciousness of those who perceive us, and, therefore,
*what we appear to be is a phenomenon — temporal, finite
and perceptible to the senses; whereas what we are, what
we have always been and what we shall always be, without
name and form, is the noumenon — timeless, spaceless,
imperceptible being.*

However convincingly you may think you have
'understood' this basic fact, you will find it almost
impossible to dis-associate yourself from the identification
with your name and form as an entity. This can happen only
when that which you have been thinking of as a separate
entity has been totally annihilated. This is the second
fundamental, the power of Maya. What is merely a
phenomenon, without any independent existence of its own,
is considered to be 'real', and efforts are made by this
phantom to 'become' something — a shadow chasing its
substance. Whereas actually you have all along been the
substance and never the shadow in bondage wanting
liberation. How very amusing, but then that is Maya!

Now the third fundamental: Would you have been able to
conceive any aspect of the manifested world if there were no

'space-time'? If phenomena were not extended into space and given a three-dimensional 'volume', and if they were not measured in duration, you could not have conceived, let alone perceived, anything of the apparent universe. Please note that all phenomena are mere appearances in space-time, conceived and perceived in consciousness. And even the very idea of the wholeness of the Absolute can only be a concept in consciousness! When consciousness merges in the Absolute, who or what can there be to want to know anything, or to experience anything?

And now the final fundamental: If what I have said so far is clearly understood, should it not be possible for you to apperceive your true state, the state before 'you' were 'born'? Could you go back to that primal state, before consciousness spontaneously arose and brought on the sense of presence? This latter state of the 'sense of presence' is true so long as the body exists. When the life span of the body is over, this conscious presence merges into the original state where there is no consciousness of being present. *No one is born, no one dies.* There is merely the beginning, the duration and the end of an event, objectified as a life-time in space-time. *As phenomenon there is no entity that is bound* and *as noumenon, there can be no entity that needs to be liberated.* This is what is to be apperceived: The dream-world of phenomena is something to be merely witnessed.

The visitor bowed before Maharaj and said that he had received the highest knowledge in the fewest words. "Having learnt about my true identity, I have nothing else to learn now." he added.   ●●

25

What are We, Really?

The normal practice at the sessions of Maharaj's talks is to wait patiently for him to start the discussion. Sometimes he would begin by talking on a definite subject; at other times he would sit silently with his eyes closed for a while and then begin to mumble softly, perhaps thinking aloud. Then again, he might at the very beginning ask the visitors if any of them had any questions. Sometimes, not too often, it happens that there is a visitor who is extremely keen to ask a particular question concerning a specific problem. Maharaj seems to sense the eagerness of such a visitor, looks directly at him even if he happens to be sitting in the last row, and asks him if he has any questions.

One morning, when Maharaj asked if there were any questions, one visitor put his hand up and started speaking. He said: Maharaj, I have a question which has baffled me so much that I am at the end of my tether. I have done a fair amount of reading on the philosophy of Advaita, and its basic tenets have impressed me deeply indeed. I have been told repeatedly by different masters that unless I give up the concept of my separate entity liberation cannot be attained. I do wholeheartedly accept that one who believes in the concept of duality — self and the other — is the one who is in 'bondage'. But I am also told that there can not be 'bondage' for anybody, because everyone has always been free! This contradictory position is difficult for me to understand. I cannot 'do' anything because no 'entity' is supposed to exist. How do I then carry on in this world? Please, Maharaj, this is not an idle, academic question. I am deeply concerned, and the problem is driving me mad. *What are we, really?*

Maharaj fixed his luminous gaze on the visitor's eyes, which, by then, were brimming with tears. He took a deep breath, sat for a while with his eyes closed, a posture which must have induced a sense of peace within the heart of the questioner. When Maharaj opened his eyes he found the visitor sitting still, his eyes closed. After a few moments, when he opened his eyes he found Maharaj smiling at him.

Well, said Maharaj, what were you thinking about during the last few moments? The answer was: Nothing. That, said Maharaj, is the answer — 'nothing'. When you said 'nothing' what exactly did you mean? Did you not mean that conceptualization, which goes on in consciousness all the time, had ceased temporarily, as it does when you are in deep sleep? Does it not strike you that the culprint is consciousness, the source of all conceptualization? Does it not strike you that the problem has been created in consciousness and cognized in consciousness, and that it is this consciousness itself which is trying to understand its own nature? Does it not strike you, therefore, that it would be virtually impossible for you to understand *conceptually* what you really are?

Now then, let us proceed. You used the would 'really'; what are we 'really'? The average person would use the word 'real' to mean something that is perceptible to the senses. The body is perceptible to the senses but would the body be 'really' you? We must use the words correctly, in spite of all their limitations. We consider as 'real' anything that is perceptible to the senses, and yet every imaginable 'thing' that is sensorially perceptible must pass through an interpretation by the mind before it is cognized. And anything that is thus cognized is obviously only an appearance in the consciousness of the cognizer. If whatever is sensorially perceptible is only an appearance, where then is the reality of the physical form which seems so very 'real' and tangible?

Should we not then go further back — at least conceptually — to the state that prevailed prior to the appearance of this physical form, this psychosomatic apparatus; prior even to the conception of this form? If I were to ask you to tell me something about your state before you were conceived in your mother's womb, your answer must necessarily be "I don't know." This 'I' who does not know that state (in fact the 'I' who knew nothing until consciousness appeared), is what we really are — the Absolute, the noumenon, spaceless, timeless, imperceptible being; whereas, relatively, phenomenally, finite, timebound, perceptible to the senses, is what we appear to be as separate objects.

The state of non-manifestation, the noumenon, is one where we (strictly, the word should be not 'we' but 'I') do not even know of our *being-ness*. When we become conscious of our beingness, the state of unicity no longer prevails, because duality is the very essence of consciousness. The manifestation of that-which-we-are as phenomena entails a process of objectivization, which is necessarily based on a division into a subject which is the perceiver or the cognizer, and an object which is the perceived or the cognized.

The interesting point about this process of objectivization is that it does necessarily take place in consciousness, which is the source of all conceptualizing, and, therefore, in effect, the so-termed cognizer-subject and cognized-object are *both* objects phenomenalized in consciousness like dream-figures. But, that cognizer-object (which cognizes the cognized-object) assumes the identity of the subject as a separate entity — a 'self' — and gives the cognized object an identity as the 'other'. Thus is born the concept of the 'individual' through illusion, the power of the Māyā, or whatever.

Once this identification with a supposed separate entity takes place, the concept of duality gets broadened and the conditioning becomes stronger. The separate subject-entity then sets itself up as an arbiter to analyze and criticize various objects, and the entire scheme of inter-related opposites comes into existence — good and bad, big and small, far and near — providing scope for condemnation and approbation.

The sub-stratum of the entire creation of this phenomenal

universe is, of course, the concept of space-time. Space is needed for objectivization and time to measure the duration of this extension in space. Without space how could objects have been given forms to become visible, and without time (duration for the appearance) how could they have been perceived?

Now, Maharaj asked the visitor, have you got the answer to your question?

The visitor, who was listening with rapt attention, as if mesmerized, suddenly realized that Maharaj had asked him a question. He was so overwhelmed by what had been imparted to him, that, for quite some time he could not utter a word, for he seemed to be enveloped in pure listening which eludes words. He was *en rapport* with Maharaj.

Maharaj continued: If you have apperceived what I have said, you should be able to say exactly how and where the so-called bondage arises, and whom it hurts. Understand this very clearly. Manifestation of phenomena is nothing but the process of the functioning of consciousness, where there is *no question of an individual entity*. All are objects, dream-figures functioning in their respective roles. Our miseries arise solely through accepting responsibility by 'taking delivery' of our respective dream-roles as ourselves, by identifying what-we-are with the subject-cognizer element in the process of objectification. It is this illusory and totally unnecessary identification which causes the 'bondage' and all the resulting misery to the illusory individual.

Once again now: *What-we-are-not is only a concept, and this concept is seeking what-we-are.* The conditioning — the misunderstanding — can only be got rid of by a proper understanding of what-we-are and what-we-are-not. It will then be clear that the 'bondage', and the 'individual' who suffers thereby, are both mere concepts, and that what-we-are, the noumenon, can manifest itself only as total phenomena. You will find peace — or, rather, peace will find itself — when there is apperception that what we are searching for cannot be found for the very simple reason that

that which is searching and that which is sought are not different!

The visitor continued to sit with hands folded, eyes closed, tears flowing down his cheeks. He was in a state of a rapturous silence more eloquent than words.   ••

26

Life, a Slapstick Comedy

One evening a visitor started the talk with these words: Maharaj sometimes says that the entire manifestation is an illusion, like a movie, or a stage play, and that. . .

Maharaj interrupted him with a laugh and said: But, it is not the usual purposeful movie; it is a hell of a comedy, a real slapstick, if you would only clearly see the whole thing as it really is. Look, here I am, in my home, bothering no one, doing what comes to me naturally. Suppose, one day a policeman suddenly appears at my doorstep and charges me with assault and robbery in Calcutta on such and such a day. I tell him that I have never been out of my home town, let alone being in Calcutta and taking part in an assault and robbery. The conviction with which I tell this to the policeman makes him a bit diffident. He conducts further inquiries and finds that what I said was true. He then apoligizes to me and leaves me alone. This is as it should be.

But here comes the comic part. You also face a similar charge; you also have never been to Calcutta, but you are so much overawed by the presence of the policeman that you are unable to speak in your defence and you allow him to arrest you. Later, when you are behind the bars, you lament about your bondage and cry for liberation! Is this not ridiculous?

In my original state of unicity and wholeness, I did't even know that I existed. And then one day I was told that I was 'born', that a particular body was 'me', that a particular couple were my parents. Thereafter, I began accepting further information about 'me', day after day, and thus built up a whole pseudo-personality only because I had accepted the charge of being born although I was fully aware that I had no experience of being born, that I had never agreed to be born, and that my body was being thrust on me. Gradually, the conditioning became stronger and stronger and grew to such an extent that not only did I accept the charge that I was born as a particular body, but that I would, at some future date, 'die' and the very word 'death' became a dreaded word to me signifying a traumatic event. Can anything be more ridiculous? By my Gurū's grace, I realized my true nature, and also realized what a huge joke had been played on me.

The more startling illusion, therefore, is not so much the happening of an event known as birth-life-death over a period of what is known as 'time', as is the acceptance of an objective entity which is supposed to undergo the experience of this conceptual event. And the basic illusion, which makes this illusion possible, is the concept of space in which objects could be extended, and the concept of time (duration) in which the spatially extended objects could be perceived.

Now, do you understand why I said that life is a slapstick comedy, a farce? Go a step further and see the extent to which your conceptual entity gets itself involved in this farce. You not only fail to see that you are merely an actor playing a role in this farce, but go on to assume that you have a choice of decision and action in the play (called 'life'), which must obviously unfold strictly according to the pre-written script. And when events thus take place naturally in the ordinary course, this conceptual entity that man is, lets himself get affected by them, and suffers. And then he thinks of 'bondage' and 'liberation'.

Liberation is seeing the life as a farce, and perceiving that you (the 'I' without the slightest touch of objectivity) can not be an entity of any shape, name or kind. Liberation is apperceiving that sentient objects are part of the manifestation of the total phenomena, without separate identities, that what 'I' am is the sentience in all sentient objects, the conscious presence as much. Liberation is apperceiving that I, the Absolute, in my phenomenal expression, am the functioning (seeing, hearing, feeling, tasting, smelling, thinking) without the presence of any other individual actors.

Now, do you understand why you 'suffer'? Because you are a case of mistaken identity; or rather because you have accepted what is obviously a mistaken identity!   ••

27

Mis-identification is 'Bondage'

One of the visitors put a question to Maharaj rather hesitantly. Being not too sure how elementary his question might sound, he said that if the problem of 'bondage' and 'liberation' really resulted from the sense of identification with the body, how and why did this identification come about. He further added (perhaps deciding that since he was going to be 'in for a penny' he might as well be 'in for a pound') that he could not understand why one should have spiritual knowledge at all, if at the end of one's life the result is the same in the case of both the Jnānī and the ignorant; the body goes back to the five elements and consciousness becomes Nirguṇa.

Sometimes Maharaj listens to the questioner with his eyes closed, particularly if he is speaking in Marathi. Maharaj listened to this visitor also with eyes closed, but as he listened expressions on his face kept changing. He looked stern and I thought that he would snap back and say: "What kind of a question is this?" But soon the sternness changed into sweet reasonableness and Maharaj smiled.

He then started speaking softly, eyes still closed: Let us first deal with the fundamentals, he said. The entire manifested universe is an appearance in consciousness. If you are not conscious, the world does not exist for you, since you can not cognize anything. This consciousness (in which one cognizes the phenomenal universe), is all that we are. As long as we are in the phenomenal world, we can perceive only that; *we cannot be that-which-we-are until we wake up from the dream of phenomenality,* understand the dream as such, and stop conceptualizing and objectivizing. This is the basic essential: *Noumenon is the substance, the phenomenon is mere reflection* — they are *not* different.

The next point to understand is this: In the phenomenal world when 'you' see 'him', both are objects seen by each other as appearances in consciousness. But, do understand this, there is no subject that sees the other as an object. There is only *seeing,* which is functioning as an aspect of the noumenal potential. This applies to everything else — hearing, touching, tasting etc. All is essentially 'functioning'.

Now, let us proceed further: This 'functioning' takes place through the medium of the physical form, the psychosomatic apparatus which as a phenomenon is itself only a manifestation and, therefore, also an aspect of noumenon, as shadow is of the substance. So long as there is no question of

an individual entity assuming choice of action, all
phenomenal functioning takes place spontaneously and the
question of 'bondage' and 'liberation' does not arise.

But, what happens is that the functional core of a
psychosomatic form (we might call it the 'personal'
consciousness for our analysis, although consciousness
cannot be divided as such) gets bestowed with a spurious
subjectivity as a separate entity, although it is itself only an
object with the noumenon as the only subject. Thus is
created the pseudo-entity that is supposed to be born, to live
and die. This pseudo-entity is also supposed to have
independent authority to choose and decide; and, with this
assumed independent authority is also assumed the
responsibility for all that would happen in the functioning of
the manifested world i.e. the suffering in this world, the
anticipated sins and merits, and the consequential 'bondage'
and the need for 'liberation'.

Is the position now clear? *What-we-are mistakenly
identifies itself in relativity with what-we-are-not,* the latter
being the pseudo-entity. 'Bondage' arises from this
identification. It is this pseudo-entity that suffers guilt and
bondage and seeks liberation. 'I' cannot possibly suffer
because 'I' is not equipped with any instrument with which
sensation could be experienced. Any experience, pleasant or
unpleasent, could only be experienced by the mis-identified
phantom object called 'me'.

Now, finally, understand what happens in the case of the
Jnānī. The Jnānī has apperceived the basic illusion of the
manifested universe as well as his *apparent* role as a
phenomenon in the spontaneous functioning of the
manifestation. He has adapted himself smoothly to whatever
may happen to the phenomenon as it goes through its
allotted journey of life, and thereafter 'returns home'. He
seems to be living his life like any other man, but the
significant difference is that he has dis-identified himself
from the pseudo-entity, and, therefore, does not experience
suffering.

In case of the ignorant person the pseudo-entity (itself an

illusion) continues to go through the dream-world, that
manifestation is, as an independent entity with apparent
volition. And it suffers because it involves itself in the notion
of causality, known as Karma, including the concept of
re-birth.

The Absolute Noumenality manifests itself through
millions of forms which are created and destroyed every
moment, and in this spontaneous functioning there is no
place at all for the notion of any entity. Therefore, any action
— positive or negative — based on the notion of an
autonomous, independent entity implies a fundamental
failure to grasp the essentials of Advaita. So long as there is a
pseudo-entity considering itself a seeker and working
towards 'liberation', it will continue to remain in 'bondage'.
It must be deeply, intuitively perceived that the seeker is the
sought. When this happens, the seeker disappears.   ••

28

You are Timeless

One morning as Maharaj climbed up the stairs to his
loft-room, he started talking even as he was taking his seat. A
few visitors had already gathered but he did not seem to take
notice of them.

Someone in the household had apparently complained to
Maharaj about the unpunctuality of somebody who had
failed to do something on time. So, time became the subject

of his talk. He began abruptly by observing that many people take time to be a 'thing' — something apart from themselves, something through which they, as individual entities, must pass. This idea is totally erroneous.

Addressing the people present, he said: Your whole idea of time is that you were born in the past, that you are now in the present (although, strictly speaking, there is no 'present' as such, because the 'present' never stays still!) and that you are growing older into the unknown future. Have you ever thought how fallacious this concept is? Is there really any past-present-future in the objective sense? The 'past' has gone beyond recall and the 'future' you can know only when it has become present-past and faded into a memory. It should be clear, therefore, that 'time' does not have an objective existence in your lives and that, therefore, it cannot be physically analyzed!

Maharaj continued: How then are you concerned with time? You are concerned with time only in so far as it denotes duration, a span of measurement, a concept. Duration signifies temporality, which is the *sine qua non* of all phenomena, including all you's and me's. Thus, *what you appear to be, what you are conditioned to think you are but are not, is temporal.* But what you *are* as Conscious Presence (and the knower of this consciousness) is intemporality. The 'past' is only a memory and the 'future' only a hope. *It is only the 'present', the now, that means anything to us, as presence is what we are as intemporality.*

I wonder, Maharaj said, if you understand what I am saying. Do you grasp the significance of what I have said? In effect what I have said is that you are time: *What you think you are, is duration, time; what you subjectively are, is timeless.* Does it startle you to be told that what you think you are is time? As a phenomenal object, are 'you' not time — the river of time flowing from infancy to old age, from birth to death, from creation to destruction, like any other manifested phenomenon? What you think you are (the psychosomatic apparatus) is always in movement, even in sleep moving towards waking, for the simple reason that

consciousness, the nature of which is movement, will not let
you be still. This constant 'doing' becomes the infamous
Karma only because of the identification with the physical
form whereby you assume the responsibility for apparent
action and, of course, for the consequences also. Each such
apparent action gets extended in space/time in order to
become perceptible in manifestation and thereby becomes
an 'event'. The entire phenomenal world represents
millions of you's. And the totality of all such action-events of
all the you's presents the world in action. The word 'birth'
should really refer to time because if duration were not born
(inseparable with 'space'), manifestation and perception
could not have taken place. *You think you were born, but
what was born was duration in which you as an object have
become perceptible.*

At the relative level, everything has to have an
inter-related counterpart in order to have even a conceptual
(if not objective) existence, but all such inter-related
counterparts like light and darkness, knowledge and
ignorance, good and bad etc., eternally separate in
conception, become inseparably re-united when
superimposed in mutual negation. Also, the phenomenally
conceived opposites, Time and Intemporality, become
re-united in the mutual negation of the relative, i.e.
wholeness, whole (soundness!). It is this basic, essential
unity which is the true perspective. Lose this perspective
and you lose your balance and fall into the abyss of Māyā.

Whatever we may think or say about the Intemporal
Absolute, concluded Maharaj, could only be conceptual,
merely an indication, a pointer, which could never possibly
reveal to us what intemporality is, because that is what we
are. All we can say is: I am *here* and *now* 'here' being in the
absence of space and 'now' being in the absence of time.
Even saying this is perhaps saying too much. It is not the
saying nor the hearing that matters. *What matters is the
instant apperception of the fact.*   ●●

29

No Such Thing as 'Enlightenment'

Maharaj often says that very few of those who come to him are novices in spiritual knowledge. Generally they are those who have travelled far and wide in quest of knowledge, read many books, met many Gurūs and have a certain idea of what it is all about, but rarely a clear vision of what they have been seeking. Many of them do not hesitate to acknowledge that all their efforts proved unrewarding and they felt frustrated and disappointed. And there are some who even wonder if they have been chasing a mere will-o'-the-wisp. However, in spite of all their frustration and dejection, they do seem to know that life does have an ultimate meaning. Maharaj feels deeply concerned for such visitors and takes personal interest in them. But he totally ignores those who come to him out of an idle curiosity, or with the object of talking about him at a weekend party with a holier-than-thou attitude or perhaps with condescension.

Then, there is a class of people — the half-baked intellectuals — who come to Maharaj to test their own accumulated 'knowledge'. And when answering Maharaj's usual query about their spiritual background, such persons seldom fail to mention with a sense of pride the long list of books they have studied and the sages and saints they have met. Maharaj receives such information with an impish chuckle and might say something that would inflate their egos even further. For example, he might say: Well then, we should have an unusually good conversation today. Or, he might say: Well, I must say we are all honoured today by your presence and we should be able to learn something new. Or, he might say: I have only studied up to the fourth standard in a primary school, and here you are, a Ph.D in philosophy, with all the Upanishads at your fingertips; how gratifying!

Discussions, as they proceeded, would have a wide range of reactions from these worthy luminaries. Some of them would start from the standpoint that they considered themselves to be more or less on the same level as Maharaj himself. Then, within a few minutes, the enormous difference would be so palpably obvious that they would adopt an attitude of humility and listen rather than talk. They would soon realize the hollowness of their pedantry and speciousness of their pet theories and concepts.

One morning, a European lady came to Maharaj. She effusively praised the book *I Am That* and said that it was her great good fortune that she was able to pay her respects to Maharaj in person. She had travelled far and wide and met many spiritual teachers, but had never felt that she had found what she was looking for, and that she was now sure her search had finally ended at Maharaj's feet. Apparently she had had a few 'experiences' which other Gurūs had probably certified as proof of her spiritual 'progress'. She began narrating these experiences to Maharaj in great detail.

Maharaj listened to what she was saying for a few minutes and then interrupted her by asking: Tell me, who had these experiences? Who felt pleased by these experiences? In the absence of what, would these experiences not have arisen at all? Exactly where do *you* figure in these experiences? Over this fairly long period of spiritual training, what is the identity you have been able to discover as *you?*

Do not please feel for a moment, said Maharaj, that I intend to insult you, but you really must get clear answers to these questions before you can decide whether you are proceeding along the right lines. At the present juncture you are like a five year old child who has been decked in fine clothes and lovely ornaments. The same child three years earlier would have either ignored the fine clothes and ornaments, or would have accepted them as a nuisance forced on her by her doting parents. But now, after the conditioning that she has received in the meantime, the child cannot wait until she can go out and gloat over the envy of her little friends who don't possess such fineries. What has happened between infancy and childhood is exactly that which is the obstacle to your seeing your true nature. The infant, unlike the child, still retains its subjective personality and identity. Before the conditioning it refers to itself by its name, treats itself as merely an 'object', not as 'me', the cognizer/subject. Think deeply on what I have said. *Personal 'entity' and enlightenment can not go together.*

If, after what I have told you, you still decide to continue to visit me, I must warn you, Maharaj said jocularly, you will not only not acquire anything, but you will lose whatever you have 'acquired' with so much effort over the past many years. What is more, you will even lose your self! So be warned! You will, if you continue to visit me, come to the conclusion that there is no 'me' or 'you' to seek enlightenment, *indeed that there is no such thing as 'enlightenment'. The apperception of this fact is itself enlightenment!*

The lady sat lost in thought. The superstructure of make-believe that she had built so assiduously over the years was shaken to its foundations. She folded her hands in obeisance to Maharaj and sought his permission to visit him daily as long as she was in Bombay.

You are welcome, said Maharaj.   ●●

30

What were You before your 'Birth'?

One of the new visitors to Maharaj was an American, not more than twenty five or so, with his head shaven — a strapping tall young man, well over six feet and proportionately broad of frame, a thin longish face with chiselled features and wearing the ochre robes of one of the many religious sects in India.

He said that he was a wandering monk and had travelled widely over most of the northern India during the last year or two. He had had the usual disciplinary training earlier for about three years. In answer to a query by Maharaj whether he had found what he was looking for, he laughed and said that he had started having doubts if he could ever find it by merely wandering about, and indeed that he now wondered if he had not been walking away from *it*.

He then said that he had come across a copy of *I Am That* recently, and after reading it, had had an unusually sharp sensation of having 'arrived'; especially when he saw the frontispiece picture of Maharaj. When he had looked into the eyes of Maharaj, he added, he could't take his gaze off the portrait for a long time. He felt he had to visit him, pay his respects, and sit at his feet.

Maharaj: What is it that you really want? Are you clear about it? Are you looking for God? What exactly are you looking for?

Visitor: Somehow, I have always known and felt deeply that nothing that life in this world could offer would satisfy me because it was all so transitory. What exactly do I want? Well,

I want to reach reality. That is what I want.

M: (Shaking with silent laughter) If you could only realize how funny that is — "I want to reach reality." Who is this 'I' who wants to reach reality? Is it this body-complex, this psychosomatic apparatus that wants to reach reality? And is he sure that 'reality' is agreeable to accept him? Also, how will this 'I' 'reach' reality? By taking a high jump or a long jump? Or, perhaps by a rocket? Or, is it through a mental leap that this reality is to be reached? And, finally, what exactly do you mean by the 'reality' that you want to reach?

V: (Laughing) Now that you put it this way, it does seem funny, or, should I perhaps say tragic.

M: Who is it that listens to these words, whether funny or tragic?

V: Me. I, the one who is sitting here; I am listening to these words and also speaking to you.

M: The respective senses, with the aid of the Prāṇa, the life-force, do the actual work. But is there not something — call it your sense of presence — without which none of your senses would be able to cognize anything? What is it that gives sentience to a sentient being?

V: Yes. If I were not conscious, my senses would not work.

M: Understand then, that *it is this conscious presence that you are, so long as the body is there*. Once your body is gone, along with the vital breath, consciousness also will leave. Only *that which was prior to the appearance of this body-cum-consciousness, the Absolute, the ever-present is your true identity*. That is what we all really *are*. That is reality. It is here and now. Where is the question of anyone reaching for it?

What were you before your 'birth'? In that state were there any needs wants, desires — even the desire for reality or freedom, or liberation? In fact, that is your original, true state or true nature — a state of wholeness, of holiness, of absolute presence and relative absence. A reflection of that state is consciousness, or I-am-ness, or being, but the reflection of sun is not the sun. This Conscious Presence is what you are, not the body which is merely the habitation for consciousness in its manifestation. When the body 'dies', consciousness is released out of the body and you are no longer even the conscious presence, because then there no longer is any relative presence. You are then in the original Absolute Awareness. *Relative absence means Absolute Presence,* without consciousness of being present.

The desire for freedom, which arises in the heart of the seeker in the initial stages, gradually disappears when he realizes that he himself is what he has been seeking. The persistence of this desire implies two 'blocks'. One, it assumes the presence and continuance of an entity wanting 'freedom', whereas for a phenomenal object there can be no question of freedom because an object does not have any independent existence at all. Two, this desire is based on the desire to capture reality at the mind-level; it means trying to capture the unknown and unknowable within the parameters of the known! It cannot be done.

V: What Sādhanā is done to do, then?

M: Here again, doing Sādhanā means assuming the existence of a phantom. Who is to do Sādhanā and for what purpose? Is it not enough to see the false as false? *The entity that you think you are is false. You are the reality.*

Once it is understood, or rather, apperceived intuitively, that an entity is purely a conceptual notion, what remains is merely a re-integration — Yoga — in universality. Nothing remains to be done because there is no one to do it, and, more important, no one to abstain from doing it either! What remains is pure non-volitional 'being lived' because relatively we are only puppets in a dream-world being manipulated in the original dream. It is for the individual dreamer to awaken from his personal dream. And this apperception is itself the awakening!

The young American, who had heard Maharaj with rapt attention, bowed before him and said: "Sir, your words have swept away all my mental debris. I now know what reality is. I know, I apperceive, I am the reality". ●●

31

Maharaj on Himself

This was one of those evenings when there were only a few of the regular visitors. Maharaj sat in his usual place, still as a statue. It was extraordinarily peaceful in that little room, and we sat there, with eyes closed, spontaneously in a state of rapport with Maharaj. Time stood still as it were. Then suddenly we heard Maharaj talking softly: I wonder what image the visitors have about me, he said. I wonder if they realize, truly apprehend, my state which, basically, is not in any way different from their own.

All I am, all I have always been, and will be, is what I was before I was 'born'. Not being a body, how could I have been born? Being Awareness itself, how could I be aware of awareness? I am no 'thing' and know no 'other', to be aware of.

As the noumenon, I am not aware of awareness. As a phenomenon I am 'functioning', an aspect of my potential as the noumenon functioning on an impersonal level, spontaneously, non-volitionally. I am, therefore, the seeing, the hearing, the perceiving, the knowing, the doing, of all that is being seen, heard, perceived, known and done — 'I' apperceiving the objectivization of this-here-now.

Noumenally (absolutely) unknowable, phenomenally (relatively) I become an object of knowledge. Noumenon-I-is what remains after all phenomena are totally negated. *I am this-here-now, total phenomenal absence. How then can I, noumenon, be known, experienced, cognized?* When I manifest myself it is as 'sentience', by conceptual extension in space, measured in duration (time). Any experience can be experienced only in duality, as subject-object, discriminating and judging through interrelated counterparts like joy and sorrow.

When the mind is totally silent, empty, when space-time conceptualizing is in suspension, then *all that you are I am* — unicity, wholeness, holiness, humility, love. That is truth — all else is rubbish! So simple, but I wonder how many apprehend what I am saying. *Stop conceptualizing and 'you' are 'I'* — no self and no other! ••

32

A Personal Experience

It is not unusual for Maharaj, during the course of a session, to pick out someone from the regular visitors and ask him about his personal reaction to his talks. He might say: Tell me what specifically you have gathered from my talks that has remained firmly in your mind. Or he might ask: Having heard what I have to say, what firm conclusion have you come to in regard to your true identity? It has been my experience that whatever Maharaj says is always spontaneous, and that it is pointless therefore to try to think of specific reasons why he puts such queries and why to particular persons.

The immediate reaction to such a query from Maharaj is naturally one of bewilderment, but understandably it is also tantamount to a confession that after listening to what he has been saying (Shravana), adequate independent meditation over it (Manana) has not been done, let alone being one with the conviction arrived at (Nididhyāsana) — the only graduated process Maharaj recommends whenever he is pressed to recommend some 'action' by a devotee.

On one such occasion, Maharaj said to one of the regular visitors: You are a learned man, and you have been listening to me now for quite some time, very patiently, very intensely, with deep concentration. Tell me in a few words what it is that I consider as the core of what I am trying to convey. Maharaj seemed to be particularly interested in the answer for he waited patiently for it for quite some time. The devotee concerned made visible efforts to give an answer, but somehow or the other a clear-cut exegesis would not come forth. During this intervening lull, so extraordinarily still and quiet, an answer spontaneously emerged in my mind: *Awakening cannot take place so long as the idea persists that one is a seeker*.

When the session was over and the other visitors had left, only my friend Mullarapattan and I remained with Maharaj; I mentioned to him that a clear answer to his question had come to my mind while we were waiting for the devotee to reply, but that I had not deemed it proper to say anything during the session. On being asked, I told Maharaj what my answer was. He asked me to repeat it, and I repeated the answer more slowly and clearly. On hearing it, Maharaj sat for a moment or two with his eyes closed, a smile on his lips, and seemed very pleased with the answer. Then he asked Mullarapattan what he had to say about my answer. Mullarpattan said he had no particular comment to make, and the matter was left at that. It seemed rather a pity, for if there had been a comment from my friend, Maharaj would almost certainly have favoured us with at least a brief dissertation on the subject.

There was another occasion which had special significance for me personally. Whilst I was doing the translation at a session, I was suddenly interrupted by Maharaj. I must mention here that on some days my translation seemed to emanate more smoothly, more spontaneously than on other days, and this was one of those occasions. While I was speaking, perhaps with my eyes closed, I was not aware of any interruption from Maharaj and it was only when my neighbour tapped on my knee firmly that I became aware of Maharaj asking me to repeat what I had just said. It took me a moment or two to recollect what I had said, and at that instant I felt myself curiously transformed, out of context, into a distant and almost disinterested witness to the dialogue that followed between Maharaj and me. When after a while I was back in the relevant frame of reference, I found Maharaj sitting back with a contented smile while the visitors seemed to be gaping at me in an embarrassed manner. The session then proceeded to its normal conclusion, but my translation thereafter seemed to me to be rather mechanical.

I felt, that something unusual had happened during the session. Unfortunately, Mullarpattan was not present on that day and I could not ask him about it. I therefore borrowed a tape-recording of the session. The recording, however, was very poor in quality and the questions and answers were drowned in outside noises. But the tape had served my purpose because, as I was meditating when the tape was being run, what transpired at the session suddenly flooded back into my memory. No wonder the visitors seemed startled out of their wits! I had been having a dialogue with Maharaj and talking to him on terms of full equality, which could never have happened if I had been really conscious of what I was saying. It was not the words but the tone of firm conviction that must have startled the visitors, as indeed I myself was when I heard the tape. I could only take some satisfaction and consolation from the fact that at the end of the dialogue, Maharaj seemed perfectly happy and contented, one might even say gratified.

The dialogue between Maharaj and me had taken place on the following lines:

Maharaj: Would you repeat what you just said?

Answer: I said, "I am the consciousness in which the world appears. Everything and anything that constitutes the manifested world can therefore be nothing other than what I am, absolutely."

Maharaj: How can you be 'everything'?

Answer: Maharaj, how can I not be everything? All that the shadow is can never be anything beyond what the substance is. Whatever is mirrored as an image — how can it be anything more or less than that which is mirrored?

Maharaj: What is your own identity then?

Answer: I can be no 'thing'; I can only be everything.

Maharaj: How do you exist in the world then? In what form?

Answer: Maharaj, how can I possibly *exist* with a form as '*an I*'? But I am always present absolutely; and as consciousness relatively, in which *all* manifestation is reflected. *Existence can only be objective, relative, I can not therefore have a personal existence.* 'Existence' includes 'non-existence', appearance and disappearance — duration. But '*I' am always present.* My absolute presence as Intemporality is my relative absence in the finite world. No, Maharaj, there is nothing egotistic about it (perhaps Maharaj had raised his eyebrows). In fact, it is only when the ego collapses that this can be apperceived. And anyone can say this — only, there is no 'one', who can 'say' this. All there is, is apperception.

Maharaj: Very well, Let us proceed.

The talk then proceeded and I continued to translate the visitors' questions and Maharaj's answers till the session came to an end. Later, I reflected upon the theme of bondage and liberation, as expounded by Maharaj, and tried to clarify its implications for me in my daily life. I recapitulated to myself what I had imbibed, something like 'chewing the cud', an expression that Maharaj uses not infrequently.

When the Impersonal Consciousness personalized itself by identification with the sentient object thinking of it as 'I', the effect was to transform the 'I', essentially the subject, into an object. It is this objectivizing of pure subjectivity (limiting the unlimited potential), this false identity which may be termed 'bondage'. It is from this 'entity-fication' that freedom is sought. Liberation therefore can be nothing other than the apperception, or immediate understanding of the false as false, the seeing that self-identification is false. Liberation is seeing that it is only the consciousness seeking the unmanifested source of manifestation — and not finding it because the seeker himself is the sought!

Having understood this profoundly, what are its implications for 'me' in regard to ordinary living? My basic understanding now is that there never can be any individual entity, as such, with independent choice of action. Therefore, how can 'I', in future, entertain any intentions? And, if I cease to have intentions, how can there by any psychological conflicts? In the absence of intention there can be no psychological basis for any involvement with Karma. There would then be perfect alignment with whatever might happen, an acceptance of events without any feeling either of achievement or of frustration.

Such living would then be non-volitional living (an absence of both positive and negative volition, an absence of both deliberate doing and deliberate not doing), going through 'my' allotted span of life, wanting nothing and avoiding nothing, so that this 'life' (this duration of consciousness which has come like an eclipse on my original true state) will disappear in due course, leaving me in my absolute presence. What more could (the conceptual) 'one' want?   ••

33

There is No Perceiver, Only Perceiving

One morning, when a visitor began his question with the usual: "I want to know . . .," Maharaj began to laugh and without waiting for the Marathi translation interrupted with a counter-question in English: "I — who"? Then, having enjoyed the joke hugely, he went back to his native Marathi and said: It is really so very simple, this that I am trying to convey to you. You too would find it so, if only you could keep the 'me' aside, when you listen! If you would only remember that so long as there is a supposedly autonomous entity, volitionally trying to understand what I am saying, true understanding is out of question. Apprehension of metaphysical revelation presupposes an enquiring, open, 'vacant' mind in which such apprehension could enter. Any 'independent' entity indicates a conditioned mind, full of concepts, resisting the entry of anything that I want to impart. Do I make myself clear, I wonder!

Even though I use words, and you hear them, the imparting will be possible only if the subject and the object merge in the hearing of it. Begin at the beginning and examine whether there exists any 'one' either to talk or to listen, or there is merely 'functioning' — talking, listening, apprehending, experiencing.

When you think of something 'existing', you think only in terms of something which is objective, with a form. You are concerned only with objective phenomena, whereas I see all objects, including you, as nothing more or less than appearances in consciousness, and therefore as not existing.

And, subjectivity as such, without any objective quality, obviously cannot exist. So then, *what exists?* There cannot be such a thing as existence or non-existence!

Let us come back to the visitor who wanted to ask some question a little while ago. He has come here, perhaps with some inconvenience and at not inconsiderable expense, to seek that kind of knowledge which would enable him to turn himself into 'a better individual' — a sage, a Jnānī. Now do you understand why I could not help laughing — not at him, please, but at the tricks Māyā plays through her illusions.

Think for a moment: Who is thinking in terms of transformation, changing from one state to another; in terms of self-improvement? Surely, it is nothing other than an appearance in consciousness, a character in a movie, an individual in a dream — a dreamed pseudo-entity considering itself subject to the workings of Karma. How could such a dreamed character 'perfect' itself into anything other than its dreamed self? How could a shadow perfect itself into its substance? How could there be any 'awakening' from the dream, except for the dreamer to re-solve the true identity of the source of the dream, the manifestation?

And 'awakening' consists in apprehending that there is no individual perceiver of the phenomenal world, but that the essential nature and purpose of all phenomena is merely the *perceiving* of phenomena, that is, *functioning in this-here-now*; apprehending that every sentient being — I — as the potential source of all experience, experiences the apparent universe objectively through a psychosomatic apparatus. The very first step in understanding what this is all about is giving up the concept of an active volitional 'I' as a separate entity, and accepting the passive role of perceiving and functioning as a process.

Let me gladden your hearts by giving you a couple of 'tips'. Inspite of whatever I say, I know you will continue on your 'self-improvement' course and keep looking for 'tips'. So open your note books and write them down:

(a) Make it a habit to think and speak in the passive tense.

Instead of 'I see something' or 'I hear something', why not think the passive way: 'something is seen' or 'something is heard.'? The perception will then be not on the basis of an action by the phenomenal entity, but on the basis of an event or occurence. In due course, the pseudo-entity 'I' will recede into the background.

(b) Before going to sleep at night, spend about ten minutes sitting relaxed both in body and mind, taking your stand that 'you' are not the body-mind construct but the animating consciousness, so that this idea will inpregnate your being throughout the period of your sleep.   ••

34

The Immaculate Identity

At the beginning of a session, Maharaj enquired: What shall we talk about today? Most of those present had attended many previous sessions and they knew that Maharaj generally selected the subject himself. Then again there was not much choice of subject either for, as Maharaj himself has said many times, he talks only on one subject — namely, man's true nature or identity. So, one of the visitors asked him if there is something to which one could hang on in order to remain constantly conscious of one's true identity.

Maharaj laughed and said that that was the whole trouble.

Some 'one' wants some 'thing' to which he could 'hang on' in order to achieve something! Can you not understand that this whole idea is misconceived? Actually, it is all very simple if you could only see it. But I am afraid the usual kind of seeing will not do. The usual kind of seeing — the seer seeing something — is totally inadequate. It needs a very special kind of seeing, intuitive seeing, 'in-seeing', wherein it is seen that there is no one to see and there is nothing to be seen!

No, he continued, I am not trying to confuse you. The subject itself is such — without substance, and yet so very full and pregnant that no other subject can have any value beside it! I could, however, give you a formula to which you can hang on, but it can only help you if you remember what I have told you about the in-seeing. If you accept it merely as a formula, you will get only the words of the Mantra, but not its meaning; perhaps the meaning of the Mantra, but not its efficacy. The real purpose of the formula, or the Mahā-Vākya, is to surrender the seeing to Brahman.

Remember always, the *perfect identity of this-that-I-am* and *that-that-I-appear-to-be*. Never for a moment forget that non-manifestation and manifestation, the noumenon and the phenomena, the Absolute and the Relative are not different. Manifestation is not a creation of the non-manifest, but merely the mirrorization, or an expression of it. In other words, there is no inherent duality between subject and object; indeed, no object could exist even for a moment apart from its subject and *vice versa*. *This-that-I-am* (noumenon) obviously transcends *that-that-I-appear-to-be* (phenomena), but is also immanent therein. There is an inseparable identity between the noumenon and its phenomena.

What happens in manifestation? Noumenally, *I am* (though not aware of it), and never for a moment do I cease to be *this-that-I-am*. Whereas phenomenally, I neither am nor am not because all objects are merely appearances in consciousness, images in a mirror. Indeed, every single thing that one can cognize can only be an appearance in con-

sciousness, and cannot have any other existence as such.
And what is consciousness? 'I' am consciousness. As soon as
the thought *I am* arises, 'mind' (which is nothing other than
the content of consciousness) starts the process of objectifying; it can do so only through the concept of duality, a
notional separation into subject and object, into interrelated
counterparts and contrasts like pleasure and pain. During
this process, noumenally, intemporally, the purely subjective 'I' remains unsplit, whole, holy and eternal as ever. In
conceptualization, in order to be cognizable, the appearances, the objects have to be given two notions without
which they would not be sensorially perceptible; they
would need to be given shape or volume in space, and
duration in time, so that they could be cognized.

If you can remain anchored in the immaculate identity
between the noumenon and the phenomena, which is your
total potential, there cannot exist any basis for the imaginary
bondage from which you want to be released. Understand
this well. Your notion of bondage is just the illusion that you
are an autonomous entity, subject to temporality and the
Karma cause-effects. If, however, you have apperceived
your basic and essential identity of intemporality, you cannot fail to see that the space-time element (the basis of the
notion of the Karma cause-effect and the consequential bondage) is essentially only a contrivance to make sensorial
perception of the phenomena possible, and cannot, therefore, be anything independent as a means of bondage.

Once again, then: *the relative manifestation — the world
— is not 'illusory'* as it is the expression of the Unmanifested
Absolute, which is immanent therein; *what is indeed illusory is your mistaken identity with a particular
phenomenon.* **Remember:** The shadow **cannot** be there
without the **substance** — but the **shadow is not the**
substance.   ●●

35

Total Absence of the Do-er

Among the visitors, one morning, was a professor of philosophy from the northern India. He had met Maharaj several times. This morning he was accompanied by a friend of his, an artist of some merit, but apparantly not particularly interested in what Maharaj speaks about.

The professor started the discussion. He said he was so struck by what Maharaj had told him during his last visit, that every time he thought about it he felt a surge of vibrations through his body. Maharaj had told him that the only 'way' to go back was the way by which he had arrived, and there was no other way. This sentence, said the professor, struck a deep chord within him leaving no room for doubt or query. But subsequently, when he began to think more deeply about the matter, especially the 'how' of it, he had found himself hopelessly entangled in an unholy mess of ideas and concepts. He said he felt like a man who had received the gift of a precious diamond but had later lost it. What was he to do now?

Maharáj began speaking softly. He said: Please, understand. *No truth remains as truth the moment it is given expression. It becomes a concept!* Add to it the fact that in order to communicate with each other, the words 'I' and 'you', and 'we' and 'they' have necessarily to be used. Thus, the very first thought breaks the unicity and creates duality; indeed it is only in duality that communication can take place. Words themselves further expand the dichotomy. But that is not all. Then the listener, instead of directly and intuitively perceiving what is being communicated, begins the process of relative reasoning with its implicit limitations when applied to the subjective and the noumenal.

Are you with me so far, Maharaj enquired, and then continued. What is relative reasoning? It is the process of reasoning whereby a subject creates in his consciousness objects with opposing qualities or characteristics which could be compared. In other words, the process just cannot work except on the basis of a subject-object duality. Such relative reasoning may be effective, and indeed necessary, for describing objects by comparison. But how can it work with the subjective? That which conceives — the subject — obviously cannot conceive itself as an object! The eye can see everything else except itself!

Is it any wonder therefore, said Maharaj, that you have found yourself bogged down in the mire of ideas and concepts from which you find it impossible to extricate yourself? If you could only see the actual position, you would see what a joke it is!

This is the background. Now, to the real problem: Who is this 'you' that is trying to go back the way he came? No matter how far back you go chasing your shadow, the shadow will always precede you. What is meant by going back? It means going back to the position when there was total absence of consciousness. But — and this is the crux of the matter — so long as there is a negator who keeps on negating and negating (chasing the shadow), 'you' will remain un-negated. Try to apperceive what I am saying, not with your intellect, not as 'you' using your intellect, but just apperceiving as such.

I wonder if I have made myself clear, asked Maharaj.

Just then I happened to look at the artist friend of the professor and was struck by the intensity of his concentration. Instead of being bored, or only mildly interested, he was listening to every word of Maharaj as if hypnotized. Maharaj also must have noticed this because he smiled at him and the artist, without uttering a word, folded his hands in salutation and nodded his head several times in a gesture of silent communion.

The professor, however, seemed to have come to a mental

obstruction, an impenetrable block, and he said so. Maharaj then told him that this 'block' was an imaginary obstruction caused by an imaginary 'you', which had identified itself with the body. He said: I repeat, there must be a final and total negation so that the negator himself disappears! What you are trying to do is to understand what you *are* by means of a concept of 'existence', whereas in reality 'I' (you) *neither am, nor am not, 'I' am beyond the very concept of existence*, beyond the concept of both the positive and the negative presence. Unless this is understood very profoundly you will continue to create your own imaginary obstructions, each more powerful than the earlier one. *What you are trying to find is what you already are.*

The professor then asked: Does it mean then that no one can lead me back to what I am? Maharaj confirmed that that was indeed so. You are — you always have been — where you want to be led. Actually, there really is no 'where' that you can be led to. Awareness of this obvious position is the answer — just the apperception; nothing to be done. And the tragic irony is that such awareness and *apperception can not be an act of volition*. Does your waking state come about by itself, or do you awaken yourself as an act of volition? Indeed, the least effort on 'your' part will prevent what otherwise might have happened naturally and spontaneously. And the joke within the joke is that your deliberately *not* doing anything will also prevent it happening! It is simple really; 'doing' something and 'not doing' something are both volitional efforts. *There must be a total absence of the 'do-er'*, the total absence of both the positive and the negative aspects of 'doing'. Indeed, this is true 'surrender'.

When, at the end of the session, the professor and his artist friend were leaving, Maharaj smiled at the artist and asked him whether he would be coming again. The artist paid his respects most humbly, smiled and said that he could not possibly avoid it, and I wondered who had had the real benefit of the talk that morning, the actively articulate professor with his learned intellectuality, or the passively receptive artist with his sensitive insight. ●●

36

No 'One' is Born: No 'One' Dies

Maharaj must have been thinking about the subject as he climbed up the steps to his loft-room. He started talking about it as soon as he had taken his seat and settled himself. This was not unusual.

He said people these days are so much enslaved by the gross utilities of life that they hardly have the time to observe themselves critically. They wake up in the morning and immediately start planning the day's activities. For activity to them is a virtue and contemplative thought a sort of dead fish. If such self-imposed pressure were avoided, they would find it most interesting to watch the process of awakening. They would notice, for instance, that between the period of the deep sleep, when they are not conscious of anything at all, and the time when they are fully awake, there is an interregnum when consciousness is just stirring and the mind weaves its fantasies into a light dream that ends when they are fully awake.

What is the first thing that happens when you are awake? asked Maharaj. Have you ever really experienced it? And observed it? If you were asked, Maharaj continued, about the first thing that happens when you are awake, you would probably be inclined to say that you see the objects in the room. Every object has a three-dimensional form, which is perceived by a 'you'. What is it that perceives the form of an object? Whatever perceives the form of the object must surely exist prior to the object perceived. You can perceive the various objects, including parts of your own body, which are also objects to whatever it is that perceives. Therefore, that which perceives is not the body, which is only an object since it also can be perceived. The perceiver is the subject and thing perceived is the object.

What is it that perceives? It is the consciousness, the being-ness, the I-am-ness, that is the perceiver. As soon as you wake up, if you were not in so much of a hurry to get up and go about your daily routine, you would notice that waking in fact means distinctively 'being present' i.e. conscious of being present, not as a particular individual with such and such a name, but *conscious presence as such*, which it is that gives sentience to a sentient being and enables the various senses to function.

You would then realize that there are two notional, but distinct centres. There is this spot of consciousness on behalf of which you instinctively say 'I', and there is the objective centre of the psychosomatic apparatus which acts in the world, with which you mistakenly identify yourself with a particular name. One is subjectively *what-you-are* as 'I', the other is a physical form which is *what-you-appear-to-be* as 'me'. Actually, there are no 'me's and 'you's, only 'I'.

Understand this profoundly — and be free; free of the mistaken identity.

Then there is the final step to be apprehended. This consciousness is the 'such-ness', the 'taste' of the essence of food of which the body is made and by which it is sustained. To that extent, consciousness too is time-bound like the body. When the body 'dies', consciousness disappears like a flame when the fuel is exhausted. Indeed, consciousness is duration, without which an object would not last long enough to be manifested and perceived. What then, are 'you'? So long as the body exists, you are this conscious presence within, the perceiving principle; when the body dies, 'you' are the Absolute Awareness into which the temporal consciousness merges. And then there is no longer the sense of being present. Remember, therefore, that no 'one' is born and no 'one' dies, because *all the forms* (that appear, remain for the duration and then disappear), *are your expression, your mirrorization.*   ••

37

Analyzing Thought

Maharaj wants visitors to ask questions, but he insists that they should not be at the level of the body-mind identification. Such questions and problems, he says, concern one's behaviour and conduct in this world about which hundreds of books have been written and there are scores of Gurūs who pride themselves on their ability to deal with them.

At one session, when Maharaj invited questions as usual, a visitor asked a question which immediately brought a warm answering smile from him, signifying that the question was well-taken and appropriate. The visitor said: Maharaj has often said that anyone wanting to be 'awakened' must eschew thought. And yet all thought cannot surely mean conceptualizing, which, one supposes, is what is to be avoided. For instance, Maharaj's answers to questions are generally so appropriate and yet so spontaneous that it might seem that there is no thought behind them, yet some thought must surely be the basis of those answers.

Maharaj said: There is indeed a great difference between thoughts and thoughts. Thoughts which form day-dreaming, or thoughts of regret about the events in the past, or thoughts of fear and worry and anticipation regarding the future are surely very much different from the thoughts which spring up spontaneously from the depth of one's psyche, what one might call thoughts that do not need any argument and interpretation by the mind. The former are to be ignored and avoided; the latter are incapable of being ignored or avoided, because they are essentially spontaneous and im-mediate and basically non-conceptual.

Maharaj then continued: The very first thought 'I am' is surely a thought, but one that does not need any argument or confirmation from the mind. Indeed, as the basis of all further thought, it is the pre-conceptual thought — very source of the mind. Living according to indirect or mediate thought, in a divided, dualistic mind is what most people do because they have identified themselves with a pseudo-entity that considers itself as the subject of all action. But direct or absolute thought is the process by which the Absolute non-manifest manifests itself. Such thought is spontaneous and instantaneous and therefore, without the element of duration which is an aspect of the split mind. Whenever there is duration the thought must necessarily be an after-thought, interpreted phenomenally and dualistically.

No spontaneous, non-dual, intuitive thought can arise unless the storm of conceptual thinking has subsided and the mind rests in a 'fasting' state; and such thought obviously cannot know bondage. Instantaneous, pure thought results in pure action without any tinge of bondage, because no entity is involved.

Maharaj concluded his reply by saying that most religions were originally based on direct pure thoughts. In course of time they degenerated into concepts. And on these concepts has been erected gradually an enormous amorphous structure, made enchanting enough to attract and mislead millions of people. ●●

38

Beingness is God

What several visitors notice after listening to Maharaj for some time is that he rarely uses the word 'love' in his exposition of the true nature of man. In fact, he often says that in the process of manifestation of the unmanifest there is nothing religious or devotional as such.

Should a visitor specifically ask Maharaj whether love had no place in what he expounds, he would smile and ask a counter-question: What do you really mean when you use the word 'love'? What significance does the word have for you? This question would generally make the visitor speechless because this word is one of those which are hopelessly misunderstood and freely misused.

Maharaj would then continue: Does not the word 'love' basically signify 'a need' of some kind, for you love the person, or the thing that satisfies your need? Indeed, the love between man and woman satisfies the need of each for the other whether the need be physical, by way of companionship, or in any other form or manner. When one finds that the other no longer satisfies the need, 'love' first turns to indifference and later on perhaps to 'hate'. Why do couples change partners, wedded or otherwise, so often, particularly in the West? For the simple reason that they no longer seem to satisfy each other's need as they did earlier.

One visitor, who wanted to pursue the enquiry further, asked some questions.

Visitor: But sir, this is definitely a narrow view of the word 'love'. There must surely be something like impersonal or 'universal' love?

Maharaj: Ah! Let us be clear what we are talking about. Are we talking about a sentiment, a relationship between two persons? If so, can love be really anything other than the inter-related opposite counterpart of 'hate' — both being feelings that one person has for another? Such a relationship can only occur in a dualistic manifestation of subject-object. If, however, you are thinking in terms of noumenal non-manifestation, which is a state of total subjectivity, (without the slightest touch of anything objective), something which can only be suggested by the subjective pronoun 'I', total unicity, which can be conceived only as a state of fullness, wholeness, holiness, no words can be adequate. And, of course, in that state a love-hate relationship would be quite inconceivable. Relationship between whom? If, therefore, you are using the word 'love' to indicate the noumenal state, this word, like any other word, would be totally inadequate.

V: Honestly, I had not considered the matter so deeply, so analytically. Perhaps what I had in mind was something that is conveyed by the words 'God is Love', or 'Love is religion'.

M: (Laughing) Here again, my friend, what are these but combinations of words based on someone's concept which he liked and wished to thrust on others? And the 'others' are more than willing to accept any concept which gives them some sort of moral moorings. In such cases the seeker is happy and complacent in his pose of the seeker. He feels so much superior to others, 'misguided souls who are wasting their lives'. And in this pose of 'enlightenment' he is happy to hang on to a concept, based on a pleasing combination of words, that feeds his seeker-ego!

V: But Maharaj, the words 'God is Love', and 'He that dwelleth in love dwelleth in God and God in him' were used by St. John, a great Christian saint, who is also believed to have been a Jnānī.

M: I do not doubt that he was a Jnānī. But unfortunately, there does not seem to have been a clear apprehension amongst his followers of what these beautiful words meant to the Christian sage who uttered them. What St. John had in mind was certainly not that 'God' is an objective, phenomenal entity whose essential nature is love.

Now, let us go back again to what I told you about need being the basis of love. Consider what is the most priceless possession of any sentient being. If he had the choice of possessing either all the wealth in the world or his 'beingness', or 'consciousness' (you may give it any name to add to the thousands that have already been heaped upon it), that which gives him the sense of being alive and present, and without which the body would be nothing but a cadaver, what would he choose? Obviously, without consciousness, all the wealth in the world would be of no use to him. This beingness, this conscious presence that he is, is the beingness of every sentient being on the earth, the very soul of the entire universe, — and indeed, therefore, *this-here-now, this conscious presence, cannot be anything other than God.* It is this which one loves more than anything else because without it there is no universe, no God. This, therefore, is *Presence-Love-God.* And, St. John was obviously very much conscious of this when he said 'God is Love. . . .' It is very clear that all he could have meant is that he (John) and He (God) were not different as pure subjectivity, as noumenon. And, therefore, he who is anchored in the conscious presence that is Love, that is God, 'dwelleth in God and God in him.'   ••

39

You are the Conscious Presence

One of the early visitors at a session was an office-bearer of a European Vedānta Society. Maharaj came straight to the point and asked him if he had any questions to ask, or any points to clarify. When the visitor said that he would like to listen for a while to what Maharaj had to say, before asking any questions, Maharaj suggested that since he was an office-bearer of one of the active Vedānta Societies with a fairly impressive membership, he might start the dialogue by telling us how they go about explaining this rather elusive subject to an interested new member of the society.

Visitor: Well, we speak to him first about Yogic physical exercises because a Westerner is basically interested in the well-being of his body. Yoga to him means being able to make the body do feats of physical endurance and also to achieve a high degree of mental concentration. After a course of Yogic Āsanas we proceed to tell him that 'he' is not the body, but something apart from the body.

Maharaj: This raises two questions: One, what is the starting point for even cognizing the body? In other words, is there not something within the body, in the absence of which you would not be able to cognize either your own body, or that of someone else? Two, would the teacher himself have a very clear idea about his own 'identity' as far as he himself is concerned? If he is not the body, who, or what, is he?

V: I am not sure what exactly you mean.

M: The body is only an instrument, an apparatus which would be totally useless but for the energy within, the animus, the sense 'I am', the knowledge of being alive, the consciousness which provides *the sense of being present*. Indeed, this conscious presence (not ABC or XYZ being present, but the sense of conscious presence as such) is what one *is*, and not the phenomenal appearance that the body is. It is when this consciousness, feeling the need of some support, mistakenly identifies itself with the body and gives up its unlimited potential for the limitation of a single particular body, that the individual is 'born'. This is the first point about which the teacher must himself have a firm, intuitive conviction.

The other basic aspect is that the teacher must also have a very clear comprehension of how the union between the body and the consciousness came about. In other words, the teacher must have no doubt at all about his own true nature. For this, he must understand the nature of the body and of consciousness (or the beingness, or the I-am-ness) and also the nature of the phenomenal world. Otherwise, whatever he teaches will only be borrowed knowledge, hearsay, someone else's concepts.

V: (Smiling) This is exactly the reason why I am here. I shall be here for about a week and I shall attend both the morning and evening sessions.

M: Are you sure you are doing the right thing? You have come here with a certain amount of knowledge. If you persist in listening to me, you may come to the conclusion that all knowledge is nothing but a bundle of useless concepts, and, what is more, that you yourself are a concept. You will then be like a person who suddenly realizes that his hoard of wealth has turned into ashes overnight. What then? Would it not be better, safer, to return home with your 'wealth' intact?

V: (Responding to the humour) I'll take the chance. I would rather know the real value of the wealth that I think I possess. I have a feeling, though, that the kind of wealth that I will attain after the useless wealth has been thrown out, would be priceless and beyond the hazard of theft or loss.

M: So be it. Now tell me, who do you think you are?

V: I doubt if it can really be put into words. But it would seem that I am not the body, but the sense of conscious presence.

M: Let me put it to you very briefly: Your body is the growth of an emission from the union of your parents which was conceived in your mother's womb. This emission was the essence of the food consumed by your parents. Your body is, therefore, made of the food-essence and is also sustained by food. And the sense of conscious presence which you have mentioned is the flavour, 'the nature' of the food-essence which constitutes the body, like sweetness is the nature of sugar, which itself is the essence of sugarcane. But, do understand that your body can exist only for a limited period of time, and when the material of which it is made ultimately deteriorates to an extent that it 'dies', the life-force (breath) and consciousness also disappear from the body. So, what will happen to 'you'?

V: But would the consciousness disappear? I must say that I am rather startled to hear this.

M: In the absence of the body, can consciousness be conscious of itself? Consciousness, in the absence of the body, will no longer be manifest. Then, we are back again to the starting point: *Who, or what are you?*

V: As I said before, it cannot be really put into words.

M: Of course it cannot be put into words, but do you know it? Once you express it, it would become a concept. But, though a conceiver of a concept, are you not yourself a concept? Are you not really born from the very womb of conceptualization? But who really are you? Or, if you prefer it, as I do, *what* are you?

V: I think what I am is the conscious presence.

M: You said, you 'think'! Who is it that thinks this? Is it not your consciousness itself on which thoughts appear? And, as we have seen, consciousness, or presence, is time-bound along with the body. That is why I told you earlier that it is necessary to apprehend the nature of this body plus life-force (Prāna), consciousness.

What you are is 'presence' only so long as the body, a manifested phenomenon, is there. What were you before the body and consciousness came upon you spontaneously? I say 'spontaneously' because you were not consulted about being presented with a body, nor did your parents specifically expect to have 'you' as their son. Were you then, relatively, not 'absence' rather than 'presence', before the body-consciousness state arose on whatever it was that was 'you'?

V: I am not sure that I understand this.

M: Now, look. For anything to appear, to exist, there has to be a background of absolute absence — absolute absence of both presence as well as absence. I know that this is not easy to grasp. But try. Any presence can 'appear' only out of total absence. If there is presence even of absence, there can be neither phenomenon nor cognizing. Therefore, total, absolute absence implies total absence of conceptualizing. That is your true original state. I repeat: The 'you' is born in the womb of conceptualizing. On the original state of total absence spontaneously arises a speck of consciousness — the thought 'I am' — and thereby on the original state of unicity and wholeness arises duality; duality of subject-object, right and wrong, pure and impure — reasoning, comparing, judging etc. Do ponder over this. But I am afraid this session must end now.

V: This has certainly been a revelation to me, although I have been studying Vedānta for quite some time.

M: Are you clear about one thing, that you are prior to all conceptualizing? *What you appear to be as a phenomenon is nothing but conceptual.* What you really *are* cannot be comprehended for the simple reason that in the state of non-conceptuality there cannot be any one to comprehend what one is!

V: Sir, I wish to come this evening for further enlightenment and will sit at your feet every day as long as I am in Bombay.

M: You are welcome.   ●●

40

Maharaj on Himself, again

What knowledge can I give to the people who come here seeking knowledge, said Maharaj one evening. Most of those who come here are so completely identified with their bodies that inspite of all their sincerity what I say they must surely find unacceptable. Even those who may 'sense' the subtlety and depth in the teaching may not be able to apperceive its real significance. But those who do intuitively apprehend what I say will need but one session with me.

How many will understand me if I say that —

1. I am always present because I am always absent; and I am only present when I am absent. To elucidate this, I would add that I am always present absolutely, but relatively, my apparent presence is my apparent absence as *I* (confusion worse confounded!);

2. I, who am no 'thing', is everything I am not, but the apparent universe is my self;

3. After all the you's and me's have negated one another, I shall remain as '*I*';

4. How could you love me? *You are what I am.* How could I hate you? *I am what you are*;

5. Never having been born, how could I die? Never having been bound, where is the need for me to seek liberation?

6. How can the relative judge the Absolute? The Absolute is indeed the relative when the relative no longer is relative — when the relative gives up all that makes it relative. In the absence of the physical form, consciousness is not conscious of itself.

7. What were you before you were born?

8. Preferences or differences are all conceptual balderdash. They can only appear relatively. Absolutely, there can be no appearance, and, therefore, no preferences or differences;

9. Collect all the knowledge you want — both worldly and unworldly — and then, offer it as a sacrifice to the Absolute, and so on. What will a listener think of me? What *can* he think of me? Is it not the only conclusion he could come to, said Maharaj with a mighty laugh, that I am absolutely — as well as relatively — crazy!   ●●

41

There Can't be Re-birth

The basic teaching of Maharaj deals with man and the world at large, the true nature of what the individual considers as 'himself' and the nature of the phenomenal world. The talks are always on the basis of man-to-man, and no recourse is generally to be had, either by Maharaj or by the visitors, to anything that any scriptures may say — however traditionally respectable they may be. Indeed, it is this pragmatic approach of Maharaj which is found to be transparently honest by the true seeker, who is not necessarily a student of philosophy. In other words, what someone else has said (what Maharaj often refers to as 'hearsay', or 'general belief') is not accepted as God's own truth, even if it appears in the most hallowed sacred texts. Besides other advantages such an approach prevents the possibility of questions begging questions as in the case of one believer, who while trying to convert a friend, tells him about a particular 'man-of-God' being able to converse with angels, and, when questioned about the veracity of such a claim, exclaims: Would a man who is able to talk with angels tell a lie?

The regular visitors to Maharaj are aware of the fact that he totally discards the concept of re-birth as sheer nonsense. But whenever a reference to this topic evokes such an unequivocal response from him, a new visitor is shocked beyond belief, particularly if he happens to subscribe to the Hindu religion. On one such occasion, a youngish visitor, dressed in the traditional ochre robes signifying his allegience to a certain Hindu sect, with the fires of fanaticism burning in his eyes, expressed his shock that Maharaj would not accept the theory of re-birth, the very bedrock of Hindu philosophy. He looked around for moral support but must have been a little dismayed by the indulgent smiles of understanding (but not acquiescence!) from the others.

Maharaj looked at the young Sanyāsin with a certain amount of sympathy, presumably for his misguided zeal, and said to him in an unusually kindly manner: This statement of mine about re-birth being absurd is nothing at all. You will be shocked even more if you continue to come here. I do not teach any philosophy, any religion; and I am not concerned with any traditional texts as the basis for my talks. I talk only from direct experience since my Guru opened my eyes — my spiritual eyes. It is not my intention to hurt anybody's feelings. I, therefore, constantly remind people that they are free to walk out if they do not like what they hear. What they would hear from me would be direct truth, as I have experienced it, not as people would like to hear it. I am afraid I do not cater to people's concepts.

Such an approach completely unnerved and also fascinated the young man who then humbly expressed his desire to continue to listen to Maharaj.

Maharaj then said: Have you ever really given thought to the essential nature of man? Forget what you have read, what you have been told. Have you given any independent thought to this question? I repeat 'independent' — quiet, thorough and deep thought, as if you were the only sentient being on the earth and there was no one to guide you? Or, misguide you! What are the essentials to that which you consider as 'you'. Obviously the body. But this body that is now in its prime, healthy and strong, was once only a little drop or speck of chemical matter when conception took place in your mother's womb. Think. Did 'you' do anything to be so conceived? Did 'you' want to be conceived? Were 'you' consulted? Further, and this is important, what is it that was 'latent' in that like speck of matter which was conceived, that caused it to grow into a fully developed baby with blood, flesh, marrow, bones, first in your mother's womb and thereafter in this world until it is now sitting before me discussing philosophy? The body has, during its growth, assumed various images which you have considered to be 'you' at different times, but no single image has remained with you constantly; and yet there is something which has indeed remained without any change. Is that not your sense of being alive and present, the consciousness which gives sentience and energy to the psychosomatic apparatus known as the 'body'? This consciousness is given various names: being-ness, I-am-ness, self, Ātmā, etc. and also other names like Māyā,.God, Love etc. The world exists for you only if this consciousness is there. If you are not conscious, as in deep sleep, can the world exist for you?

Now, do you get some idea of what it is that makes you instinctively think of yourself as 'you' — this composite of the physical body, the life-force (Prāṇa) which is the active principle, and consciousness which enables the physical senses to cognize things. *What you appear to be is the outer body, what you are is consciousness.*

Let us come back to your problems of re-birth. What is 'born', the objective body, will, in due course, 'die'; thereafter it will be dissolved i.e. irrevocably annihilated, the life-force will leave the body and mingle with the air outside. The objective part of what was once a sentient being will be destroyed, never to be re-born as the same body. And consciousness is not an object, not a 'thing' at all — therefore, *consciousness, as something non-objective, cannot be 'born', cannot 'die' and certainly cannot be 're-born'.*

These are indisputable facts, are they not — facts about the phenomenally manifested sentient being? As a process of the functioning of the noumenon, manifestation of phenomena takes place, in which forms get created and forms get destroyed. Who is born? And who dies? And who is to be re-born?

If this is so, you may ask how does the concept of Karma, causality and re-birth arise at all? The answer is that instead of a phenomenon being accepted as a manifestation of the unmanifest (and thus an aspect of the non-phenomenal noumenon), a mistaken identification with a pseudo-entity takes place and a phantom with a supposed autonomous existence gets created. This phantom is supposed to have choice of decision and action. It is this phantom that is supposed to be born, to live, to suffer and to die. And in this process, it is this phantom who becomes liable to the process of causality known as Karma, accepts the supposed 'bondage' and 're-birth', and seeks an imagined 'liberation'.

In other words, concluded Maharaj, over the natural process of the manifestation of phenomena gets superimposed a phantom-self with a supposed autonomous, independent existence, and on this phantom-self is loaded the concept of the resultant effects of the imagined volitional actions — i.e. Karma, bondage and re-birth!

Do you understand now why I debunk the theory of re-birth?   ●●

42

Intellect Can Be an Addiction

It is interesting to watch the gradual change that comes over a visitor who is fortunate enough to be able to visit Maharaj for even a short period of, say, only ten to fifteen days. Almost invariably the visitor (assuming, of course, that he is a genuine seeker and not someone who has come either to test Maharaj's 'level' or to show off his own) is so very enthusiastic at his first visit that he does not have the patience to sit still and absorb quietly what is being said. He is ready with his questions even before Maharaj has finished talking, as if he had already guessed what Maharaj would say.

In such cases it is difficult to anticipate the reaction from Maharaj. Generally he is very patient for a while; but sometimes, perhaps when he suspects the bonafides of the visitor, he can be very brusque and might ask the visitor to sit quietly in a corner for the first five or six days and listen without uttering a single word. As the visitor settles down gradually and is able to curb his impetuosity, he becomes appropriately receptive to the finer, subtler meaning of Maharaj's words and his whole attitude changes. When, later, Maharaj invites questions and there is no response from this visitor, Maharaj, remembering his earlier effervescence, would gently pull his leg and ask him what happened to all those questions which kept popping up earlier!

There are some visitors, however, who are not able to settle down easily. They would try, but their inherent restlessness would erupt into questions time and again as if there was an intellectual barrier that prevented Maharaj's words from reaching them.

In one such case, the visitor went out of his way to repeatedly assure Maharaj that he was not crossing swords with him, that, indeed, what Maharaj had said was so fascinating that he would have loved to be able to accept it without any question, but that would not be honest because then the doubt would remain in his mind. Maharaj assured him that he did not question his sincerity or his intentions, but that he would have to give up the 'drug' to which he had become addicted before he could be in a position to receive anything of spiritual significance. The visitor was taken aback at the use of the word 'drug' by Maharaj, and was about to protest but Maharaj continued without paying any heed.

Intellect, said Maharaj, is certainly essential for assimilation and evaluation of worldly knowledge and, of course, it is also needed up to a point for spiritual knowledge. Thereafter, what is needed is not mere intellect but an innate intuitive capacity which is a gift that some people have in better measure than others. You have become addicted to the drug named intellect and under its influence you analyze everything; you cogitate, contemplate and make simple things complicated! You have to get rid of this addiction and surrender yourself to the intuitive process of pure receptivity. Once you do so, what I give, you will receive directly without any intervention by the intellect.

A puppet can only react to the stimuli imparted by the puppeteer, but sentient beings have the capacity not only to react to the stimuli, which is what happens generally, but also to act independently of any outside stimulus. The kind of receptivity to which I refer is obtained when there is not only no reacting to stimuli, but an openness to consciousness without the intrusion of personal proclivities and set views; in short, without the intrusion of individuality.

The trouble is that you, as an individual personality, think that you are listening to what I, also an individual, am saying. Actually what is being said is being said not by me as an individual but by consciousness which has no shape or form. The listening too must be done by consciousness without the intrusion of an imaginary individual. Would it be possible for you to have any questions at all if you were not conscious? Would it be possible for me to talk to you if I were not conscious? Let consciousness listen to what consciousness says about consciousness! Do remember that all thoughts are movements in consciousness, observed and cognized by consciousness; the individual has no place in this functioning except as a mere appearance in consciousness!

The visitor bowed before Maharaj reverentially and said: Sir, I now realize that what I believed to be my castle is actually my prison.   ••

43

Seeing the False as False is Truth

At one of the sessions the subject being discussed was: What exactly constitutes 'bondage'? Maharaj explained that what we are is the noumenon — the timeless, spaceless, imperceptible being, and not what we appear to be as separate objects — time-bound, finite and perceptible to the senses. The 'bondage' arises because we forget our real being, the noumenon, and identity ourselves with the phenomenon — the body — which is nothing but a psychosomatic apparatus.

When Maharaj invited questions one of the visitors, who had attended several sessions and had hardly asked any questions earlier, put his hand up and asked: Would identification with the body — merely because of such identification — mean bondage? The Jnānīs cannot give up their bodies during the lifetime and must live their lives like other human beings so far as the physical functions are concerned. What is more, all the Jnānīs do not act in a uniform manner; each has his own way of behaving in the world, his own way of dealing with others. To this extent, is there not a certain identification with the individual body, even where the Jnānīs are concerned?

Maharaj smiled in appreciation of this well-grounded question. He said: The body is an instrument necessary for consciousness to remain in manifestation. How can the two be 'dis-identified' until the life-breath leaves the body (commonly known as death) and consciousness is released from its phenomenal form? Bondage is not caused by mere formal identification with the body, which is a psychosomatic construct of the five elements, an instrument having no independent existence of its own. What causes 'bondage' is the identification resulting in the *imagined concept of an independent, autonomous entity* which assumes the doership and thus 'takes delivery' of the actions and the responsibility for the consequences.

I repeat that it is not just the fact of identification with the body that is responsible for the concept of 'bondage'. The body must continue to be used as an instrument. Bondage can arise only when there is apparent volition, i.e. when an action is imagined to be of one's choice as a 'doer', thereby bringing into motion the process of causality, of Karma and 'bondage'.

It is necessary to understand how the apparent entity comes to be superimposed on the general process of manifestation. *Once you see the false as false, it is not necessary any further to seek the truth*, which anyway cannot be conceived as an object. At what stage does the question of identification arise? Phenomenality being integrally latent in noumenality (noumenality being immanent in phenomena) the question of identification should not really arise at all. There is no need of any specific identification between noumenality (Avyakta) and phenomenality (Vyakta) as such. Such need arises only when there is manifestation of the noumenal-Absolute in separate phenomenal objects, a process of objectivization which necessarily requires 'dualism' — a dichotomy into two elements — a subject (Vyakti) which perceives and cognizes and an object which is perceived and cognized. The important point is that both these cognizer-subject and the cognized-object are interdependent objects and can only exist in the consciousness in which the manifestation process occurs, and which consciousness indeed is what we *are!*

Do understand this basic point: We can only exist as one another's objects; and that too only in the consciousness of that cognizer-subject which cognizes us, each object taking the position of the subject-cognizer (Vyakti) *vis-a-vis* the others who become the objects. And here arises the 'entity' (Vyakti). The cognizer-subject, in considering his subjective function, assumes 'himself' as an entity, an independent, autonomous 'self' with volition and choice. This phantom-entity then further pursues the principle of 'dualism' (which is the very basis of manifestation) in order to compare, discriminate, make a judgement and choose between his objects, from the standpoint of the inter-related opposites like right and wrong, good and bad, acceptable and not acceptable etc.

It is this illusory 'entity-fication' and not merely the identification with the body, which is the root of 'bondage'. Once again: What we are, the noumenal-Absolute (Avyakta) manifested as the totality of phenomena (Vyakta) is devoid of any *individual* objective existence. Therefore, what-we-are cannot suffer any 'birth' or 'death', neither bondage nor liberation. Both bondage and the resulting suffering are, purely conceptual, based on the identification with the wholly *imaginary* subject-cognizer-entity (Vyakti).

An example of what Maharaj had said is provided by the manner in which he appreciates a good dialogue on a subject which has developed itself interestingly. When, during discussions on abstruse subjects, anyone from the audience shows a penetrating insight into what Maharaj has said, he feels delighted like a child who has received the desired toy. How well the topic has developed this morning, he might say. Sometimes, utterly oblivious of any implications to an ordinary divided mind, he might say that such a high-level discussion on Advaita would not be available anywhere else! But what may appear to be self-praise on such occasions is actually the sheer joy of self-effacement. He is then the Vyakta, and not the Vyakti.

It was said of Ramana Maharshi that when people chanted 'Hymns in Praise of Ramana', he himself would join them in the singing and keep time by clapping his hands like all the others. He had utterly disidentified himself with any entity and was, therefore, totally oblivious to any implications of his actions. The hymns referred to 'Ramana', not to an individual. The Jnānī really has no individual entity to be embarrassed about, and his psychosomatic apparatus, the body, carries out its normal functions in the normal way without his being aware of them.   ••

44

Dabbling in Meditation

One day a new visitor presented an egregious problem. Sometime earlier, a ten-day course of intensive meditation was organized by a certain Swami. This visitor had no particular interest in meditation nor any specific object in enrolling for this course, but he had got himself enrolled because some of his friends who were keen to do so wanted him to join them, and he could afford to take that much time off from his business. It is, he said, part of his character and temperament to devote his concentrated attention, with firm determination, on anything that he takes up. So, once the course of meditation started, he devoted full attention to it and conscientiously did whatever was asked of him. The result was that at a certain moment of time, towards the end of the course, he had a definite feeling of being separated from his body, and the whole world appeared to be of the nature of a dream. And that feeling had persisted ever since. It was, he said, not at all an unpleasant feeling. On the contrary, it gave him a peculiar sense of freedom. But, he added, there was a real difficulty: How was he to live in this dream-world and at the same time carry on his business and earn a living?

This was in the usual course translated into Marathi for Maharaj, but even before the translation could be completed, it was clear that he had grasped the problem and there was an expression of unusual gravity on his face. He sat still for a few moments and then started speaking: Meditation, he said, is not something one can dabble in as an experiment or entertainment, just to see what happens. A certain preliminary preparation for it is necessary.

Consciousness is the basis for all manifestation of the phenomenal world. There is no greater power on earth than consciousness; if one fools around with it, it would be impossible to foresee the consequences that may follow. And if the psyche is not prepared to face the consequences, there could be serious trouble at the body-mind level for the simple reason that there had been no earlier preparation in dis-identifying oneself from the body. What would happen if a bolt of high power electricity is shot into a receiver that is not strong enough to receive it?

Maharaj then addressed this visitor directly and suggested that he should attend his talks atleast for fifteen days. Unfortunately, however, the visitor had to go back to his town almost immediately. Maharaj obviously felt sorry for him and said that in that event he could only suggest that he should read *I Am That* attentively and that he should recall to his mind this visit as often as he could, and think of this meeting he had with him. Remember: a remembrance of what I am is the knowledge of what you are.

Maharaj added: You might see the whole Universe as a dream, but so long as there is a 'you' seeing this dream as a separate entity, you will be in trouble. Let us hope, gradually you will come to realize that you are also a dreamed figure in this living dream, an integral part of the dream, and not someone apart and separate from it. Then you will be all right.   ●●

45

There is Nothing but 'I'

Maharaj repeatedly asserts that he would not care to discuss ethics, the codes morality, the modes of conduct prevailing in society. There are many other people who have the special training, the inclination as well as the time to discuss such matters in depth and at length. He himself would keep away from the subject altogether, except, of course, to the extent that one must implicitly obey the law of the land and avoid deliberately hurting anyone by one's actions. Apart from this very general, universally acceptable minimum standard of conduct and morality, he would avoid any discussion on the finer points of the subject because, he says, the standards and criteria of morality and conduct have been changing according to times and circumstances. He would deal only with the unchangeable true nature of man himself. If one understands, apprehends one's true identity, all the rest loses its significance and importance because all subsequent thoughts and actions, not being based on duality, would be simple, direct, intuitive and spontaneous.

This view of Maharaj is found to be extremely difficult to accept, not only by the new visitors, who perhaps feel that he is shying away from the very crux of the problem of life, but also by some others who have listened to him over a long period. They find it impossible to accept the dichotomy of the two. Whatever conclusion and conviction one may come to regarding one's true nature, how can one afford not to give as much, or even more, thought to one's relationship with and behaviour towards one's fellow beings? So, when Maharaj defined his attitude in this regard at a session, one of the regular visitors, a lady, could not restrain herself from asking a rather pointed question: Maharaj, would it be right and proper for a person to listen to you most attentively, understand thoroughly what you have to say to the extent that he becomes a Jnānī, and then to go out and prepare an atom bomb and use it if he felt like it?

Maharaj promptly replied: If you had only thought seriously about this matter, keeping in mind the basic fact that you had no wants, no needs, no problems at a certain point of time — say, a hundred years ago — you would have arrived at the answer yourself; the answer being that the question itself is misconceived!

If, as you say, a person understands and accepts his true identity to the extent of being a Jnānī, would he not come to the conclusion that all phenomena, all sentient beings, including himself as a phenomenon, are nothing but conceptual images in mind, as imaginary as those in a dream? Would someone who has deeply apperceived this truth think of preparing an atom bomb, let alone using it?

But this is only a superficial answer to satisfy the ignorant. What you must find out is who are these 'me', 'you' and 'him' that we are talking about, who are supposed to be doing this or that, according to their sweet will and pleasure! How do you see yourself? You see your body — or really a part of it — and you identify yourself with it. But in deep sleep, or under sedation, you do not identify yourself with this body. What really happens is that the appearance of your body in consciousness is perceived and interpreted by you exactly as it is done by any other observer. Your own interpretation about yourself is as illusive and ephemeral as that of others, though maybe a little more flattering! The point to be noted is that the solid personality you think yourself to be is nothing more than an appearance in consciousness. What is more, the interpretation will change, and has been changing, from time to time. Any thought about yourself, whether your own or someone else's, is only a movement in consciousness, only a *temporary* mental image. That is all that you are. But is that truly you? Only a mental image? Is there really any image with which one could identify oneself as an unchangeable, independent, autonomous entity, with choice of action?

Relatively — phenomenally — 'you', or 'me' is nothing more than that speck of physical matter which was conceived in a womb and within which was latent the spark of consciousness that is immanent in the entire manifestation. The innumerable forms of phenomena in relativity are all objects of the Absolute subjectivity — 'I', the basis of manifestation being duality through a subject and object, every object being the 'other' to whichever object that is perceiving it in the capacity of a supposed subject. Not a single object has any independent existence as such. We all are mere appearances in consciousness, concepts in mind, each sentient being, being nothing more than his own concept and the concepts of those whom he considers as 'others'.

If you have no independent existence, how can you act? Do you indeed act at all? Or, do you only react to an outside stimulus like a puppet? If you would sit still and see what happens, you would quickly realize that we do not really 'live' but are 'being lived'; that life as such is nothing more than what might be called an apparent functioning — apparent because all the functioning is, again, nothing more than a panoramic appearance in consciousness. If there is no consciousness, as in deep sleep or under sedative, there is no functioning either.

Then, in all this functioning where do 'we' come in? That is the ultimate joke in this comedy of Māyā! 'We' have not only never been out of it, but the *entire functioning is nothing but us. What we are is the whole,* holy, noumenal Absolute, sensorially imperceptible, and perceived and cognized only in relative duality as manifested phenomena. 'We' are transcendance phenomenally as 'I', and immanence noumenally depending on how we see ourselves. *There is nothing but 'I', no 'me', no 'other'.* In relative manifestation, phenomena are conceptualized in consciousness as 'me', and each object, assuming subjective identity, cognizes the other objects as 'others', but noumenally, there is only the subjective 'I' without any duality.

Now let us come back to your atom bomb. If you have really apperceived this, is it possible for you to go on thinking any longer that there is any villain in life with an independent, autonomous entity, possessing enormous power for 'evil'? Or, that there is any Avatār possessing enormous power for 'good'? Are they both anything other than the drop that got conceived? Surely you must realize that 'good' and 'bad' are mere inter-dependent opposites, essential manifestations in duality, appearances in consciousness acting their respective roles in the total functioning. Indeed, believing in and identifying oneself with an entity is all the 'bondage' there is, and realizing that there can be no entity, separate from the overall functioning of Prajnā, is instant liberation.   ••

46

Negation of 'Entity-ness'

Once during the course of a session, Maharaj was explaining why death has such a traumatic terror for the average person, whereas to him it would be an experience to look forward to, as it would mean release from the limitation which the phenomenon of the body naturally imposes on consciousness. Once the body 'dies', manifested consciousness is released and merges with the impersonal consciousness like a drop of water merges with the ocean.

Maharaj sensed that a visitor had some question on this

point. He looked at him and said: "It seems that you want to ask a question." The visitor was a bit startled because perhaps he had not got down to framing a suitable question to clarify the doubt which had just stirred in his mind. Anyway, he proceeded to speak: Maharaj has said that what actually happens in death is that the breath, the life-force, leaves the body and mingles with the air outside; consciousness also leaves the body and merges with the impersonal consciousness, and the dead body is destroyed one way or another. Nothing remains of that particular physical form which was created and in due course destroyed. If this process applies both to the ignorant and to the Jnāni, where is the need to become a Jnāni?

Maharaj answered: When you talk about an ignorant person and a Jnāni and the need for an ignorant person to become a Jnāni, do you not assume that there is an independent and autonomous individual, capable of exercising personal volition according to his choice and decision? In the process whereby the phenomenal universe comes into manifestation, is there a provision for such independent entities?

What is the basic conceptual framework without which manifestation of the phenomena would not be possible? If there were not the concept of 'space' constituting volume, could an object have been apparent with the three dimensions? And, without another concept, 'time', could the appearance of an object have been perceived, i.e. without the duration in which the object could be cognized? So then, if the framework which we call 'space-time' is itself conceptual, could the objects apparent in that conceptual framework of space-time, which all human beings are, be anything other than conceptual, imaginary phantoms?

Therefore, understand firmly and once and for all, that no conceptual object, although mistaken as a separate entity, could possibly have any kind of independent existence or personal volition. *No one is born; no one dies. What is born is only a concept.* There is no entity to be freed. Not understanding this fact constitutes the bondage of

ignorance; apperception of it is the freedom of truth.
Remember, truth is absolute correspondence with reality. It
is the unshakeable knowledge of man's true nature. It is the
total negation of entity-ness.   ••

47

The Seeker Is the Sought

A European couple came to visit Maharaj for about a week.
Both husband and wife had been interested in Vedāntic
metaphysics for many years and had studied the subject
deeply. There was, however, a touch of tiredness, almost of
frustration, in their outlook and general behaviour which
clearly showed what was subsequently confirmed. They had
no clear apprehension of truth inspite of their assiduous
search over a long period of time during which they had
travelled extensively and had sought guidance from
numerous Gurūs, but without success. Now, they were
perhaps wondering, if this was going to be another exercise
in futility and more frustration!

After having given information about their background in
response to the usual question by Maharaj, they sat listlessly.
Maharaj looked at them for a few moments and said: Please
understand that I have nothing at all to give you. All that I
shall do is to put before you a spiritual mirror to show you
your true nature. If the meaning of what I say is understood
clearly, intuitively — not merely verbally — and accepted

with the deepest conviction and the most urgent immediacy, no further knowledge will be necessary. This understanding is not a matter of time (indeed it is prior to the concept to time) and when it takes place, it happens suddenly, almost as a shock of timeless apprehension. In effect it means a sudden cessation of the process of duration, a split-second when functioning of the time-process itself is suspended — as integration takes place with what is prior to relativity — and absolute apprehension occurs. Once this seed of apprehension has taken root, the process of the relative deliverance from the imagined bondage may take its own course, but the apprehension itself is always instantaneous.

The keyword in the process of understanding what I say is 'spontaneity'. The manifestation of the entire universe is like a dream, the cosmic dream, exactly like the micro-cosmic dream of an individual. All objects are dreamed objects, all are appearances in consciousness, whether it is the dream arising spontaneously as a personal individual dream during sleep, or it is the living-dream of life in which we are all dreamed and lived. All objects, all appearances are dreamed by sentient beings in consciousness.

Sentient beings are, therefore, both dreamed figures as well as dreamers; there is no single dreamer, as such. Each current dreaming of the universe is in the consciousness which is within a particular psychosomatic apparatus, the medium through which the perceiving and the interpreting occurs, and which is mistaken as an individual entity. In deep sleep there is no dream and, therefore, no universe. It is only when you use the divided mind that you exist apart from the 'others' and the world.

You have no control over the objects in your personal dream, including the object that 'you' are in your dream. Everything is spontaneous, and yet every object in your personal dream is nothing other than you. In the life-dream too, all objects (all 'individuals', even if they are opposed to one another in the dream) can only be what-you-are. All functioning, all action in life, therefore can only be spontaneous action because there is no entity to perform any action. You *are* (I am) the functioning, the dream, the cosmic dance of Shiva!

Finally, remember that all dreaming of any type must necessarily be phenomenal, an appearance in consciousness, when consciousness is 'awake', that is when consciousness is conscious of itself. When consciousness is not conscious of itself there can be no dreaming, as in deep sleep.

At this stage, there was a query from the male partner of the couple. His point was: If all of us are only dreamed-figures, without any independent choice of decision and action, why should we be concerned with bondage or liberation? Why should we come to Maharaj at all?

Maharaj laughed and said: You seem to have arrived at the right conclusion the wrong way! If you mean that you are *now* convinced, beyond a shadow of doubt, that the object with which you had identified yourself is really only a phenomenon totally devoid of any substance, independence or autonomy — merely a dreamed appearance in someone else's consciousness — and that, therefore, for such a mere shadow there can never be any question of either bondage or liberation, and that consequently there is no need at all for you to come and listen to me, then you are perfectly right. If this is so, you are not only right but already liberated! But, if you mean that you should continue to visit me only because you cannot accept that you are a mere dreamed figure, without any independence or autonomy, then I am afraid you have not taken even your first step. And, indeed, *so long as there is an entity seeking liberation, he will never find it.*

Look at it this simple way: What is the basis of any action? Need. You eat because there is a need for it; your body evacuates because there is a need for it. You visit me because of the need of visiting me and listening to what I say. When there is need action follows spontaneously without any intervention by any doer. Who feels the need? Consciousness, of course, feels the need through the medium of the psychosomatic apparatus. If you think you are this apparatus, is it not a case of mistaken identity, assuming the burden of bondage and seeking liberation? But really the questioner, the seeker is the sought!

Absolute stillness prevailed in the room as everyone pondered over what Maharaj had said. The visiting couple sat with eyes closed, oblivious of the surroundings, whilst the other visitors gradually filed out of the room.   ●●

48

The Nature of Deep Sleep

Among the many visitors who come to Maharaj, there are some who, perhaps because of an earlier common line of guidance or study, find themselves bogged down at a particular point of comprehension. They invariably seek clarification about it. For one such group of people the problem centred round the nature of the state of deep sleep.

They had understood — or more likely, they had misunderstood what they had been told — that the state of deep sleep was indeed the 'ultimate' state, or our original state, and they were quite upset to be told by Maharaj that nothing could be farther from the truth. How can the state of deep sleep, Maharaj asked them, which alternated with the waking state in consciousness, be our true state? Consciousness itself is time-bound, and it depends upon the food-body for its manifestation and sustenance. The state of deep sleep is, therefore, very much a physical condition with a duration alternating with the waking state. The reason why it is mistaken for the non-objective awareness — where awareness is not aware of itself — is that during deep sleep consciousness temporarily retires into rest. The important difference to note is that the state of deep sleep is similar to Awareness only to the extent that consciousness is then not conscious of itself. However, this state is at once 'in movement' in so far as it has a duration, after which the waking state again takes over.

All that one can say is, added Maharaj, that the sense of presence, which is present during the waking state, is absent in the deep sleep state. The state of Awareness — what we truly are — on the other hand, is the total absence of both the presence and the absence of the sense of presence. This is the all-important distinction.

It is a measure of the strength of conceptual conditioning that people who were supposed to have reached a high spiritual level (whatever it might mean!) could not easily apperceive this basic distinction which Maharaj makes between deep sleep and Awareness. It was pitiable to.see Maharaj demolishing their concepts one after another, concepts which they had held so long and so lovingly, and which they were obviously so reluctant to let go. But it was clearly necessary. With his irrespressible sense of humour, Maharaj likened the state of mind of the questioners with that of a millionaire who is informed that all his millions have suddenly turned out to be totally worthless!

Maharaj threw further light on the subject by explaining that both the waking state and the deep sleep state are alternating periods in consciousness-in-manifestation. If this is clearly understood, he said, there would be no confusion. A hundred years ago, Maharaj asked the leading member of the group, were you concerned with deep sleep? Did you need sleep? Now, when consciousness has manifested itself in a physical apparatus, could you carry on without deep sleep for any length of time? Consciousness, deep sleep, waking state, duration in time all constitute the same concept associated with manifestation. How could it possibly be equated with the Unmanifest Awareness, which is intemporality, pure subjectivity without the slightest touch of objectivity?   ••

49
Annihilation of the 'You'

Addressing the visitors one morning Maharaj said: Some of you have been coming here for many weeks. I am particularly concerned about the overseas visitors who come here only to meet me and not for sight-seeing. They have to spend a lot of money on travelling and their stay in Bombay, and I sometimes wonder if they really understand what I am trying to convey. Now, tell me, you know what Paramārtha is — the sublime truth, the ultimate meaning (of life). What is this ultimate meaning for each of you? Think over what I have been talking about before you answer.

One bold answer from a foreign visitor was: Liberation. I want to be liberated from the bondage of this life. Having heard you, I would now call it 'the bondage of consciousness'. Soon there were confirmatory murmurs from several others.

Maharaj laughed and said: Look how strong the conditioning can be! Whether the conditioning is from the parents or from the spiritual guides is not relevant. This problem of 'bondage' and 'liberation' is part of the traditional teaching that is given to those whose intellectual and intuitive level is not high enough to grasp the true essence of *that-which-is.* But you are not kindergarten students of spirituality. I keep telling you that you must cease to think and speak as if you were phenomenal objects. I have been telling you that you are not phenomenal objects, but consciousness itself, the animating consciousness which provides sentience to the sentient being; further, that you are consciousness only in manifestation, but truly *you are that which is prior to consciousness itself,* i.e. *you are Pure Awareness.*

Is it not simple enough to understand, Maharaj asked, that a mere object, an appearance — which is all that a physical body is — cannot possibly perform any action whatsoever as an independent entity? It is only when the Impersonal Consciousness, in its total functioning, manifests by objectifying itself and becomes identified with each object that the concept of the personal 'I' comes into being. This concept is the source of 'bondage', the objectivizing of 'I' the pure subjectivity, into an objective 'me'. It is this 'me' — the I-concept, or the ego — which is the imaginary bondage from which liberation is sought. A clear perception of what constitutes the sentient being that is seeking liberation will show how ludicrous the whole idea is. The body itself is nothing but the growth of the male sperm which gets fertilized in the female womb; the foetus is the essence of the food consumed by the parents, and in it consciousness is latent. If it is now clear that what we appear to be is nothing but the essence of food, may I ask, said Maharaj, which particular grain of food you want to liberate? Which particular grain of food, or which of the five elements, food being the essence of the combination of the five elements, are you identifying yourself with?

Awakening, or enlightenment, or liberation is nothing, absolutely nothing other than apperceiving profoundly, deeply, intuitively that what we are — *that-which-is-here-now* — is the absolute absence of whatever is imaginable or cognizable; which is the same as the absolute presence of the unknowable potentiality.

Just think for a moment, said Maharaj: Can any question arise which does not have at its centre a 'you' or a 'me' as an individual — seeing or not-seeing, understanding or not-understanding, doing or not-doing? It is always a 'me' that is concerned. Hardly ever is it the thing seen, or the matter understood, or the act that happens. Whenever there is Parā-Vritti, a complete and total change-over, a 'metanoesis' has happened. The change-over has not been 'done' or 'achieved' by any entity of its own volition. It is this fact that is not realized. What is not realized is that there can be no entity which has directly, volitionally caused the change-over! Indeed it is the apperception as such (not by any individual) of this very fact that brings about the essential annihilation of the 'you' — the seeker — and achieves the sort of vacuum, a 'fasting' of the mind, which invites the presence that is the real 'you' ('I', not 'me'). This is how the transformatory adjustment happens or comes about. It cannot be achieved.

Do understand, concluded Maharaj, that objects and their Guṇas (attributes) are not subject and object, as perceived by the senses and interpreted by the· mind, but that all are objects, including human beings, mere appearances in consciousness — and finally, therefore, *objects cannot and need not be 'liberated'*.   ●●

50

An Irreverent Revelation

Maharaj's daily routine includes Bhajans and prayers four times a day, the first one being as early as 5.30 in the morning. During these Bhajans one sees him deply absorbed in the verses that are chanted. Until recently he even used to sing and dance with great abandon. Now, of course, he is not strong enough to do so.

At one of the sessions, a visitor said to him: Maharaj, you may be a perfect Jnānī, but when I see you singing Bhajans with such emotion, I feel extremely happy that devotion still clings to you very firmly. Maharaj answered promptly: Everything has its place in the world as well as in our daily routine. The important thing is to understand the position as it really is, to have the right perspective. Devotion and reverence are all right so long as one recognizes them for what they are, i.e. effectivity, and to that extent a bondage. And when one sees something for what it is, it loses its force, but if one gets involved in it the bondage gets stronger and stronger. All feelings and emotions (love, devotion, etc.) are based on duality, and so long as these feelings continue to dominate one's outlook, duality will continue to have a firm hold, and the real holiness, wholeness, unicity will be out of reach. The whole position is so obvious and simple that one cannot but laugh, and even be apparently irreverent, when one looks at the fantastic superstructure of superstition and mystery that has been built on and around the basic simplicity that Truth is!

Do understand how simple and direct this is: 'I', — *intemporality* — am total awareness without being aware of this awareness; total subjectivity, without the slightest touch of objectivity. I manifest through consciousness, through duality, by means of subject and object, through the concepts of space-time and the range of inter-dependent opposites, without which manifestation and objectivization would not be possible. *All manifestation is my expression,* my mirrorization in which I manifest as each sentient being; this object, this sentient being, appears to function and considers itself (erroneously) as the subject. But 'I' am the only subjectivity and all functioning in the manifested world is my objectivization in consciousness, which indeed I am,

All phenomenal objects, aspects of what I am, become sensorially perceptible only when they are extended into what I manifest as 'space' and measured into what I manifest as 'time'.

Again, therefore, the simple and obvious truth: *This-here-now,* all manifestation sensorially perceived, is not different from what I am in my unicity. And, of course, every sentient object can say this.

Once this simple position is clearly understood, you may do what you like while going through the span of life that has been allotted to you. Indulge yourself, if you like, in devotion and reverence, sing Bhajans, but understand the false as false. Understand that there is nothing religious or reverential about the process of manifestation, which occurs spontaneously, in which you as an individual entity are in no way concerned.   ●●

51

Who Suffers?

When the number of visitors is small, Maharaj is inclined to talk in a more informal and intimate manner. But when his little loft-room is fairly well-filled, he first asks if any one has any questions, but generally adds a restrictive, or rather, a constrictive condition that the question should not relate to what one should do or not do in this world. In other words, questions should be asked without identifying oneself with the body! This restriction, it may be presumed, is intended to keep out superficial and flippant questions which would only mean a waste of time. It is also understood that people will not ask him how they should grapple with the complexities of their personal problems. Maharaj makes it abundantly clear that he is neither a soothsayer nor a miracle man.

One morning, someone asked why one has to suffer. Why unhappiness exists. Maharaj sat still for a few moments and then began to talk softly: Whatever emotion or feeling one experrences is a movement in consciousness. When one feels sorrow or unhappiness, it means that an event has not satisfied the need or want that is felt at that moment. However, the event that may cause sorrow to one individual may give happiness to another; and yet again an event that has caused unhappiness to a particular person at one time might give happiness to the same person at another time, depending on what he thinks he wants at that time. What are the factors involved in what one thinks of as the experiencing of happiness or unhappiness, pleasure or pain? One, there must be consciousness; two, there must be the concept of an entity, person, with its wants; three, there must be an event in space-time.

An event may happen and even the person with his wants may be there, but if there is no consciousness, he will not be concerned either with the event or its effect. It is consciousness which is the principal factor and the actor! Indeed, 'what-I-am' was not even aware of its existence untill the knowledge 'I am' arrived. In that original state, there was no possibility of any needs, wants, hopes, wishes, ambitions, pleasures or pains — all of these came along with the body. Even after the arrival of consciousness, what was felt was a conscious presence as such — 'I am' (not I am this, or that). It is only after consciousness had identified itself with its outer form that the notional entity came into being. And this entity is nothing but a concept. It has no independent existence of its own.

Along with consciousness comes the concept of space-time, without which manifested phenomena cannot be perceived. For manifestation to be sensorially perceptible, it must necessarily have a volume which is not possible without the concept of space; and manifestation to be extended as an event in duration, needs the concept of time. Happiness and unhappiness and all the different inter-related opposities or contraries do not really exist on their own; they cannot do so because they are nothing but conceptual objectifications in space-time. And if these contraries are at any time superimposed, they would cancel out one another and restore the balance.

What we are Absolutely (timeless, spaceless, unconditioned, totally without attributes or identity, pure being) cannot know what pain or pleasure is, because what we are has nothing at all objective about it, and only an object can suffer or have any kind of experience. What we appear to be as separate objects are manifested phenomena — time-bound, finite and perceivable through the senses. We can suffer only through our mistaken identity with the separate objects! Should we not at least understand this?

Stand back in your original state of wholeness, the state before you were 'born', when there was no knowledge *I am* and, therefore, no need and want of any kind. All suffering will end as soon as you stand apart in pure awareness of the false as false, the transient as transient. Once you see that the false and the transient depend for their very existence on the concept of space-time, you are nearer to your true being. Once you realize that it is the notional entity, which you imagine yourself to be, that suffers, you awaken into that wholeness of your true nature in which holiness and healing are implicity contained.

In conclusion, Maharaj referred to 'the vile disease with which the doctors have charged me'. The very mention of the disease — cancer — would normally put a patient into a state of shock. But my reaction is totally different: Who is ailing? Evidently, that which was 'born' will 'die' in its appointed time. In due course, the 'material' which is the source of this particular psychosomatic apparatus will become moribund owing to deterioration and will be pronounced as 'dead', and the consciousness within the apparatus will be released to merge with the immanent all-pervading consciousness. What about me? There never was a 'me' there never can be a 'me'. 'I' have always been present, absolutely. Indeed, *my relative absence will be my absolute presence,* and the moment of 'death' will be the moment of the highest ecstacy, the last sensorial perception of the psychosomatic apparatus.   ●●

52

Progress in Spiritual Search

Maharaj is always ready to deal with the doubts and difficulties of the seekers; he wants them to ask questions. He keeps telling specially the overseas visitors that since they have spent considerable amount of money and taken a lot of trouble in coming to India to meet him, they should not waste their time sitting silently but should ask him relevant questions. If you really have no questions to ask, he says, it means that you have already had the apperception of Truth; why waste your time; why don't you go home? If, on the other hand, there is some area of enquiry which is not quite clear, clarification should be obtained right here and now. "But," he warns, "Do not ask questions as a human being centred in a phenomenal object. Remember, I am not talking to individual entities, but as consciousness to consciousness about consciousness."

One of the foreign visitors, who had been coming to Maharaj for quite some time, began quietly: Perhaps I am speaking from a body-mind identity but there is a question, a problem, which has been troubling me for so long that I cannot keep it bottled up any longer. I have talked about it to some of the seekers here and I know that they too have the same problem. However, now I am not speaking for them but only for myself. The problem is: How am I to know if there is any progress in my spiritual search? Occasionally, particularly during meditation, I do have a glimpse of what I am searching for, but only a glimpse and that too only on rare occasions. How am I to know if I am progressing?

Maharaj understood the sincerity and earnestness with which the visitor had asked the question, but, inspite of his sympathy for the questioner, he could not conceal the frustration he felt. He sat still for some time, perhaps to get over the combined enervating effect of his illness and the mental anguish at being asked the question. Then he began speaking softly, more in sorrow than in anger: I think I should stop talking altogether and put up a notice to that effect! I find that many of you come here as a matter of habit, or for a new experience which your friends have mentioned to you. You don't really listen. If you did, such a question should not arise. And, if at all it did, you could have easily dealt with it yourself, in case you had listened to me attentively and understood what I had been saying. Instead, I find that this question does disturb many of you.

The problem apparently is about 'progress'. Now, who is to make the progress, and progress towards what? I have said this repeatedly and untiringly that *you are the Conscious Presence*, the animating consciousness which gives sentience to phenomenal objects; that *you are not a phenomenal object*, which is merely an appearance in the consciousness of those who perceive it. How can an 'appearance' make any 'progress' towards any objective? Now, instead of letting this basic apperception impregnate your very being, what you do is to accept it merely as an ideological thesis and ask the question. How can a conceptual appearance know whether it is making any conceptual progress towards its conceptual liberation?

Maharaj took a match box in his hand and held it up. He asked: Is this you? Of course not. Does it need time to understand this? Apperception of this fact is immediate, is it not? Why then should it take time to apperceive that you are not the phenomenal object called the body-mind? Remember, you are the animating consciousness that gives sentience to the phenomenal objects. Please understand, said Maharaj, that apperception is prior to the arrival of consciousness which is the basis of intellect. Apperception is not a matter of gradual practice. It can only happen by itself instantaneously — there are no stages in which deliberate progress is made. There is no 'one' to make any progress.

Perhaps, one wonders, could it be that the surest sign of 'progress' — if one cannot give up the concept — is a total lack of concern about 'progress' and an utter absence of anxiety about anything like 'liberation', a sort of 'hollowness' in one's being, a kind of looseness, an unvolitional surrender to whatever might happen?   ••

53

The Suffering of Experience

One morning we could see that Maharaj was physically quite uneasy, obviously due to the pain from the cancerous condition in his throat. During the last few months his suffering had become acute, though he never complained about it. Even in this condition he was not bed-ridden and was found at his seat unfailingly every morning and evening. And he did talk too, though rather briefly and in a low voice. Visitors would have to listen to him very intently, and with that special receptivity which would enable them to grasp the true meaning of what he had to convey. In fact, Maharaj felt that speaking less in a few chosen words, as he now did, was better than long expositions. Those who were true seekers would understand him even if he spoke less, for they had the right receptivity and intelligence. So it is perhaps just as well that I am not able to speak at length, Maharaj would say.

One of the visitors that morning, a lady, was very much moved by Maharaj's condition and the way he was bearing his pain stoically. She thought that physical pain could be even worse than death. She could not help telling Maharaj: Sir, I am not afraid of death, but I have a dreadful fear of physical pain. Please tell me how I could get rid of this fear?

Maharaj laughed and said: I am afraid I cannot help you there, but I am sure there are many others who know the methods of avoiding or lessening physical pain. All I can do is to explain to you what suffering itself is and who suffers.

You must always go to the root of the problem. When did the experience of suffering first start? Do you have any memory of any suffering, say, a hundred years ago? When did the experience start? Think about it deeply so that the answers to these questions would arise within yourself without any words. Is life — living itself — other than experiencing; experiencing in duration, moment to moment stretched horizontally? And what is experiencing? Is it not reacting to an outside stimulus which is interpreted through the senses as an experience — pleasant and acceptable, or, unpleasant and not acceptable. One does not experience suffering — one suffers an experience, pleasant or unpleasant.

Now, the basic question you should be concerned with is: *Who (or, more appropriately what) is it that suffers an experience?* Let me tell you straightaway: '*I*' *do not (cannot) suffer any experience, pleasant or unpleasant; it is only a* '*you*' *or a* '*me*' *who suffers an experience.* This is a very important pronouncement and you should ponder over it deeply.

I should really let you solve this problem for yourself, or rather, let the problem work itself out! But let us proceed. 'I' cannot suffer any experience, because 'I' am pure subjectivity without the slightest trace of objectivity, and only an object can suffer. A 'me' or a 'you' is an object and, therefore, suffers experience. Also, like any other object, a 'me' or a 'you' can have no substance and, therefore, can exist only as a concept in consciousness. Further, never forget that it is only consciousness which can suffer because any reaction to a stimulus, which is what experiencing is, can only take place through consciousness. Indeed, therefore, *consciousness and suffering are identical*, and not in any way different. Ponder over this very significant point.

What I say you will find rather difficult to grasp because you have identified yourself with the body, the psychosomatic apparatus through which an experience is suffered, the instrument in which the suffered experience is registered. You have lost your identity with 'pure subjectivity, the Absolute that you truly are, and have mistakenly identified yourself with the objective 'me'; therefore you say 'I suffer', and therefore you are 'bound'.

Do you understand what I have been saying? I am aware of my true identity as intemporality, infinity, subjectivity — therefore I do not and can not suffer. I am aware that it is consciousness that apparently suffers an experience through the sensorial apparatus. You, on the other hand, believe that you are the sensorial apparatus and it is this mistaken identity of yours that is the cause of your suffering and your bondage.

So long as there is consciousness functioning, keeping the sensorial apparatus working, there will also be living, experiencing, suffering — positive or negative. But you, as 'I', are only the witnessing of it all. All functioning is the objective expression of what-I-am subjectively, and every sentient being can say this: What-I-am cannot suffer any experience, only an objective 'you' or 'me' can suffer an experience.   ••

54

Words and their Fulfilment

It was a morning when Maharaj was perhaps feeling his physical weakness a little more than usual. One could clearly notice the inexorable effects of the vile illness on his body, irrespective of his indomitable spirit. He looked frail and exhausted.

He sat in his usual place, quite still, almost immobile, totally oblivious of the pain which must certainly have been intense. Then he started talking quietly, very softly; one had to concentrate a great deal to catch his words.

What you see, said Maharaj, as my presence as a phenomenon means my absence as the noumenon. Noumenally, I can have neither presence nor absence because both are concepts. The sense of presence is the concept which turns the unicity of the Absolute into the duality of the relative. *Unmanifested, I am the potential which in manifestation becomes the actual.*

I wonder, Maharaj continued, if these words really convey anything to you; are they mere words? Of course, I don't doubt your sincerity. You have come here — many of you from long distances and at considerable expense — and spend quite some time sitting on the floor, which most of you are not used to; and you certainly seem to pay attention to what I say. But you must understand that unless there is a particular type of receptivity words would only accomplish a very limited purpose. They might perhaps arouse your intellectual curiosity and titillate your desire for knowledge, but they would not open themselves up to reveal their true significance.

Now, what is this special type of receptivity? Here again

one finds the endemic limitation of communication by words. Would it mean anything to you if I said that 'you' have come here to listen to me, but you must listen to me on the basis that this 'you' is wholly illusory, that there is really no 'you', who could listen to my words and get any benefit! Indeed, I must go so far as to say that unless you give up your role of an individual listener expecting some benefit out of what you hear, words for you would be mere empty sounds. The obstruction preventing apperception is that although you might prepare yourself to accept the thesis that everything in the universe is illusory, in this illusoriness you fail to include yourself! Now, do you see the problem — or is it more a joke than a problem?

When — let me not say 'if' — you accept this basis for your listening, that is to say, you give up all concern for the listener wanting to be a 'better' individual by listening to the words and hoping to 'work' towards a perceptible improvement, then do you know what would happen? Then, in that state of intuitive listening, *when the 'listener' no longer intrudes*, words would throw up and expose their subtle, inner meaning, which the 'fasting' or open mind will grasp and apperceive with deep and instant conviction. And then will words have achieved even their limited fulfilment!

When the listener remains in a state of suspension without intruding on the listening as such, what in fact happens is that the relative, divided mind is automatically restrained from its natural proclivity to engage itself in tortuous interpretation of words, and is thereby prevented from maintaining a continuous process of objectification. It is then the whole mind that is enabled to be in direct communion with both the talking and the listening as such, and thereby to bring about the Yoga of words, enabling the words to yield their innermost meaning and their most subtle significance.   ●●

55

Confusion about Life and Death

Ever since it became known that Maharaj has been suffering from cancer of the throat, more and more people have started coming to him, even those who otherwise would perhaps not have done so. Many of them look genuinely worried. Many express their astonishment that inspite of the fatal disease, Maharaj is cheerful and vocal as usual, albeit looking pale and weak.

One evening, when people around him seemed distressed and sorrowful, Maharaj started talking about life and death. If you could only apperceive the position as it really is; he said, you too, like me, would not be concerned about life and death. Indeed, there is no difference at all between the two. Were you not 'dead' before you were born? What is darkness other than the absence of light? What is 'death' other than the absence of 'life', and more significantly, is not 'life' merely the absence of 'death'? 'Life' begins as an image in consciousness and when the image ceases to exist, we call it 'death'. The fear of death is actually a product of the desire to live, the desire to perpetuate one's identity with the illusive entity of 'I' as separate from 'you'. Those who know reality also know the falsity of 'life' and 'death'.

Maharaj continued: The basic cause of the confusion is the mistaken belief that there is an entity, an autonomous, objective entity, to experience the happenings — called 'birth' and 'death', and the duration between the two, called 'life'. In reality, all these are mere conceptual images in consciousness, which have as much substance as images on the television screen or in a dream.

Do try to understand, he continued, what phenomena are — all phenomena. They are only appearances in consciousness. Who perceives them? Consciousness itself, through the mechanism of the twin concepts of space and time, without which appearances would not have a perceivable form and could not be cognized. And the cognition itself takes place through a division of the mind (mind being the content of consciousness) into subject and object; and the reasoning and selecting process based on the duality of the inter-dependent opposites — love and hate, happiness and unhappiness, sin and merit etc.

Once this process is correctly observed, it can be easily understood that there can be no actual individual to be born, to live or to die. There is a manifestation, an appearance in consciousness, generally known as 'being born' — an illusion in space. When this manifested appearance goes through its temporal span and comes to its end, there occurs another illusion in temporality that is known as 'dying'. This simple process cannot be perceived as such so long as one persists in the notion of a 'live-er' of a life and 'die-er' of a death.

Maharaj then concluded: That 'material', or 'chemical', which was conceived in the mother's womb and which spontaneously grew into the body of a baby, grows by itself to its maximum limit, then starts decaying and finally ends by merging into the original 'material'. The breath leaves the body and mixes with the air outside; the consciousness within merges with the Impersonal Consciousness and the process of that particular 'happening' is over. *What-we-are is neither 'born', nor 'lives', nor 'dies'*.   ••

56

The Last Days: Last Teaching

Dark and dismal clouds overhung the horizon and there was the distant rumbling of thunder and lightning. We knew the storm was coming — the inexorable finality, the relentless leveller who holds nothing as sacrosanct.

Our beloved Master's vitals had been consumed by cancer and we knew his frail body would fall soon, perhaps sooner than we feared. But we were afraid of showing our fear to him for he would be hurt to find that his teaching was wasted on us. He had taught us that human beings were mere conceptual forms, no more·real than dream-figures, that it is only the body that is subject to birth and death and not the self, which is not only ageless but birthless and deathless. And he was the Supreme Self. Yes, we knew all this, and yet at the prospect of his passing away we had started feeling like orphans, for we loved him too! It was difficult to rise above the human feelings and failings!

During his last days — from May-June to 8 September, 1981, when he dropped his mortal coil, his body had visibly withered day after day, but his. spirit remained indomitable till the end. He continued to talk, though in a weak voice, with inherent authority, and at his mere word, as it were, the listeners' illusions and delusions shrivelled.

I give below verbal cameos from some of his talks during these last days. He could not speak for long; he had to be brief, but whatever he said was seminal in nature and a sort of catalyst for the listeners. It was the Great Beyond speaking, not a frail old man in the clutches of death!

For over a fortnight now — June 1981 — Maharaj has not been able to talk to visitors with his old zest. At the insistent request from many of us he has agreed to limit the discourses to a half hour, and it is just as well that he has done so, because even thirty minutes of talking has been exhausting him physically so much that he is unable to sit up thereafter.

Maharaj's words, though fewer, are more pregnant now. He has been saying that his physical weakness prevents him from elaborating what he wants to convey. He adds that this is a sort of blessing in disguise because the listeners would now have to pay greater attention to what he says, without letting their mind wander about much. Also they would do a certain amount of thinking for themselves!

Many of the visitors, in view of the extremely weak physical condition of the Master, now restrict their questioning to a minimum, even though Maharaj presses them to get their difficulties cleared up. "There's so little time now," he says.

*   *   *

One morning, one of the regular visitors, perhaps with a view to keep Maharaj's mind away from his physical suffering, started talking on various matters and asking rather superficial questions. Maharaj, of course, was quick to see through the device and sat erect in his easychair. I know what you are trying to do, he said, but you forget that I am not what you think I am. I do not suffer; I cannot suffer because I am not an object. Of course there is suffering. But do you realize what this suffering is? *I am the suffering.* Whatever is manifested, I am the functioning. Whatever is perceptible I am the perceiving of it. Whatever is done I am the doing of it; I am the doer of it, and, understand this, I am also that which is done. In fact, *I am the total functioning.*

If you have apperceived this, you need to know no more. This is the Truth. But the meaningful word is 'apperceived'. What I have said I have said for myself. But if you have apperceived this, you too can say the same thing. You and I are not two, but the same Absolute Unicity.

If this apperception prevails, you could not possibly have

any quarrel with anyone, whatever he does or does not do. Why? Because you will then have realized that whatever happens is part of the general functioning in consciousness and that no phenomenal object (which is in effect merely an appearance in someone else's consciousness) can possibly have any independence of existence or volition of action. Ponder over this deeply.

*   *   *

Another morning, Maharaj sat half-reclined in his bed, with his eyes closed. Visitors had arrived one by one and had quietly taken their seats. Seeing the Master resting, they sat in meditation with their eyes closed. It is astonishing how easy it is to go into the state of the 'fasting' mind in the Master's presence. Suddenly, Maharaj started speaking though in a very weak voice.

You people come here wanting something. What you want may be knowledge with a capital 'K' — the highest Truth — but nonetheless you do want something. Most of you have been coming here for quite some time. Why? If there had been apperception of what I have been saying, you should have stopped coming here long ago! But what actually has been happening is that you have been coming here day after day, identified as individual beings, male or female, with several persons and things you call 'mine'. Also, you think you have been coming here, of your own volition, to see another individual — a Gurū — who, you expect, will give you 'liberation' from your 'bondage'.

Do you not see how ridiculous all this is? Your coming here day after day only shows that you are not prepared to accept my word that there is no such thing as an 'individual'; that the 'individual' is nothing but an appearance; that an appearance cannot have any 'bondage' and, therefore, there is no question of any 'liberation' for an appearance.

Do you even now realize that if the very basis of your seeking is wrong, what can you achieve? Indeed, is there anything to be achieved? By whom? By an appearance?

This is not all. Whatever I say is being tape-recorded by some people; some others take down their own notes. For what purpose? To make the conditioning even more powerful? Do you not realize that there never has been any question of 'who'? Whatever has happened (if at all anything has happened) has been spontaneous. There never has been any room for an individual in the totality of manifestation; all the functioning is at the level of the conceptual physical space (Mahadākāsh), which is contained in a conceptual speck of consciousness the mental space of time, perception and cognition (Chidākāsh). This totality of the known finally merges in the 'infinite potentiality that is the timeless, spaceless Reality (Paramākāsh). In this *conceptual* manifestation, innumerable forms get created and destroyed, the Absolute being immanent in all phenomenal forms. Where do the individuals figure as individuals? Nowhere. And yet everywhere, because *we are the manifestation. We are the functioning. We are the life being lived. We are the living of the dream. But not as individuals.*

The apperception of this truth demolishes the individual seeker; the seeker becomes the sought and the sought is the apperception.

*   *   *

At another session, Maharaj brought up yet another aspect of the same theme, i.e. people coming to him wanting knowledge. This time he asked: What is this 'knowledge' that you want, this knowledge about which you take down notes? What use will be made of those notes? Have you given any thought to this aspect of the matter?

The real point is, he continued: Did you find any need of any knowledge a hundred years ago? *That, which you do not know and cannot know is your true state. This, which you think is real because it can be objectified, is what you appear to be.* Whatever knowledge you are now seeking about your true state is unknowable, because *you are what you are seeking.* All that you can get as knowledge is at a conceptual level — the knowledge that you would get as an objective appearance. Such 'knowledge' is in no way different from 'ignorance',. because they are inter-related counterparts at the conceptual level. In other words, *comprehension   at   the   mind   level   means   only conceptualization and, therefore, is totally illusory.* Do understand please, the difference between such conceptualized knowledge and the intuitive apperceiving which is not at the conceptual level. Indeed, apperceiving is whole-seeing or in-seeing, which is vitally different from mere intellectual seeing. Once there is apperception, the duality of counterparts, the basis of mere intellectual comprehension, totally disappears. There is no question of any 'one' thinking that he has understood something by the use of reasoning and logic. True understanding is spontaneous apperception, intuitive and choiceless, and totally non-dualistic. Meditate on what I have said.

* * *

One day when a visitor brought up the question of 'ethics' and moral behaviour (matters which have always been considered outside the scope of discussion here) Maharaj was so amused that, inspite of extreme physical weakness he sat up and said that he never ceased being astonished at the confusion in thinking that was displayed even by people who were supposed to be intellectuals. He literally laughed himself into a paroxysm of coughing. Once having understood that there is a separate place, the toilet, for specific purposes, would you, he asked, use the living room or the bedroom for those purposes?

Once there is an unequivocal apperception of your true nature, once you clearly see the false as false, is there any question of having to decide the propriety or otherwise of any action? Who will make the decision? Does one have the independence of volition to make the decision? Is there really any choice? Once it is apperceived that there is no entity with any independence of action, would 'living' thereafter not be totally non-volitional living? Would not, in other words, the apperceiving itself lead to an abandonment — or more accurately — a spontaneous cessation of the very concept of volitional activity? One may think that one lives; actually, one is only 'being lived'.

Exhausted by this brief but animated exposition, Maharaj lay back again in his bed, and said that he would have liked to expand this point further, but he just did not have the physical strength. He added, with a wry touch of humour, that it was perhaps just as well that he could now only give out capsules of knowledge.

*   *   *

This particular morning, Maharaj was too weak even to sit up but was in a mood to talk. He started speaking softly and slowly: What a fantastic subject this is! The subject is elusive, the person who thinks he is listening is illusory, and yet nobody believes that he does not exist! When you come here, I welcome you and extend to you my humble hospitality, but in doing so I am fully aware of the exact position, i.e. there is neither a speaker nor a listener. Why is it that nobody can honestly say that he does not exist? Because he knows that he is present — or, rather, there is that intuitive *sense of presence* — and, this is important, there is no entity who can say that it does not exist. If an entity did assert that it did not exist such an assertion itself would prove its existence!

However, the more important point which is not so easy to grasp, is that the source of this phenomenal presence (which is the manifestation of the unmanifested) is noumenal absence. Further — I wonder how many of you would apprehend this — it means that whenever the mind is 'fasting', totally without any conceptualization, there is phenomenal absence, and this presence of phenomenal absence is noumenal.

*   *   *

It was a Sunday and Maharaj's small room was packed to capacity. Most of the visitors were regular ones, but a small group had arrived from a distant part of the country. The leader of the group discerned Maharaj's effete physical condition and reconciled himself to the fact that they would have to be satisfied with Darshan only. Maharaj however sat up in his bed, looked directly at the new group and smilingly asked if there were any questions. He added that he was not at all well physically and hoped that the questions would be at an appropriate level. There was a brief murmured consultation among the group, and the leader very respectfully said that he had only one question to ask: Is there really such a thing as 'enlightenment'? He added that this question was being asked not frivolously but against the background of a long spiritual quest. Maharaj smiled and started talking inspite of the exhaustion which was clearly visible on his face. He sat up quite erect and his voice gained an unexpected vigour.

Notwithstanding my repeating it constantly, he said, even the regular visitors do not seem able to accept the fundamental fact that it is sheer nonsense to think of an individual's need for enlightenment. Basically, there is only 'I'; there is no 'me', or 'you', to be enlightened. How can a phenomenal object, which is only an appearance, be transformed by 'enlightenment' into something other that what it is, i.e. a mere appearance?

When 'enlightenment' occurs, there is an apperceiving that what we believe to be our normal condition — that of a phenomenal object — is merely a temporary condition, like an illness, which has come over our normal true state of the noumenon. It is suddenly realized that what was being considered 'normal' was not really normal. The result of such apperceiving is a sort of instantaneous adjustment from an individual existence to *just existence as such;* volition disappears and whatever happens seems right and proper. One takes one's stand as the witness of all that happens, or rather only witnessing remains.

*   *   *

This morning Maharaj lay in bed, obviously in the no-mind state. For several minutes, the visitors — not too many, it being a working day — sat still. Suddenly the Master opened his eyes, and said very softly that there would not be any talk because he was too weak to speak. But he smiled graciously and added very slowly: If you would only apprehend, deeply and intuitively, what you were before you acquired this body-cum-consciousness, say a hundred years ago, even from within this physical prison, you would be seeing the world without the sense of duality — not from your identity as an illusory individual centre. Conceptualizing would cease.

Then the Master waved a hand to indicate that the session

was over, and the visitors dispersed.

*   *   *

Sunday, 12 July 1981 — As is usual these days Maharaj was lying in his bed, his legs being massaged by his faithful devotee and attendant, Anna. His breathing was rather laboured, mostly through the mouth, and he seemed almost fast asleep. Then suddenly he was struggling to sit up and was helped to a reclining position, leaning heavily against propped up pillows. He started speaking, and his voice was surprisingly firm. What I want to tell you is astonishingly simple if only it would be apperceived. And the amusing part of it is that it can be apperceived only if the 'listener' is totally absent! Then, only apperceiving remains and *you are that apperceiving.*

What happens is that the unmanifest Absolute expresses itself in manifestation: Manifestation takes place through millions of forms; consciousness functions through each form, the conduct and working of each form being, *generally,* according to the basic nature of the category to which the form belongs (whether it is a plant, or an insect, or a lion, or a man), and *particularly,* according to the nature of the particular combination of the basic elements in each form.

No two human beings are alike (the fingerprints of no two persons are exactly alike) because the permutations and combinations of the millions of shades of the eight aspects (the five basic elements and the three Gunas) result in billions and trillions of forms, the nature of no two forms being exactly alike. Millions of such forms are constantly being created and destroyed in the process of manifestation.

A clear perception of this process of manifestation comports the understanding: (a) that there is really no question of any identification with any individual form because the very basis of this manifestation-show is duration (of each form) and *duration is a concept* of time; and (b) *that our true nature is the witnessing of this show.* It goes without saying that the witnessing can take place only so long as the show goes on, and the show can go on only so long as there is consciousness. And who is to understand all this? Consciousness, of course, trying to seek its source and not finding it, because the seeker is the sought. Apperceiving this truth is the final and the only liberation and 'the joker in the pack' is the fact that even 'liberation' is a concept! Now, go and ponder this.

After speaking these few words Maharaj felt totally exhausted. He lay back in bed. In a feeble voice he added: What I have said this morning is all the Truth anyone need know.

*   *   *

Tuesday, 14 July 1981 — A group of three was visiting Maharaj for the first time. Although languishing in bed and extremely weak, Maharaj asked the group if they had any questions. They had a brief talk amongst themselves and decided on asking only one question: "Maharaj, all three of us have done certain Sādhanā for some time, but the progress does not seem to be adequate. What should we do?" Maharaj said that the purpose of any effort is to get some thing, some benefit which one does not possess. What is it that you are trying to achieve? The answer was quick and positive: We want to become like you — enlightened.

Maharaj laughed and sat up in bed. When he was made a little more comfortable with a couple of pillows to support his back, he continued: This is where the misconception lies; thinking that you are an entity who must achieve something so that you can become like the entity that you think I am! This is the thought which constitutes 'bondage', identification with an entity — and nothing, absolutely nothing, other than dis-identification will bring about 'liberation'.

As I said, you see yourselves and me as entities, separate entities; I see you exactly as I see myself. *You are what I am,* but you have identified yourself with what you think you are — an object — and seek liberation for that object. Is this not a huge joke? Can any object have independent existence and volition of action? Can an object be bound? And liberated?

The questioner joined his hands in a Namaskār and most respectfully submitted that what Maharaj had said could not possibly be challanged as a theoretical ideal, but, surely, he said, even though people may be fictitious entities, nothing more than mere appearances in consciousness, how are we to live in the world, unless we do accept the different entities as 'real' enough in life?

This discussion seemed to give an extraordinary zest to Maharaj, and the feebleness in his voice gradually disappeared. He said: You see how subtle this subject is. You have provided the answer in your own question, but it has eluded you. What you have said in fact is that you *know* that the entity as such is totally fictitious and has no independence of its own; it is only a concept. But this fictitious entity must live its normal life. Where is the problem? Is it so very difficult to lead a normal life, knowing that living itself is a concept? Have you got the point? Once you have seen the false as false, once you have seen the dual nature of what you call 'life' — which is actually *living* — the rest should be simple; as simple as an actor acting his role with zest, *knowing* that it is only a role that he is playing in a play or a movie, and nothing more.

Recognizing this fact with conviction, apperceiving this position, is all the truth. The rest is play-acting.

*   *   *

Thursday, 16 July 1981 — There were only a few regular visitors present. Maharaj, although visibly tired and exhausted, demanded that someone should ask some question, or give a talk! So, someone started with these words: "The consciousness that I have. . . . ."

If it were one of the occasional visitors who had said this, Maharaj would probably have ignored the implication of what was being said. But this was a 'regular' who should have known better. Maharaj suddenly shouted "Stop". Inspite of his debilitated condition, the word was like the sound of a gun shot. He glared at the speaker and said: What do you mean by saying: "The consciousness that I have. . . . .?" Do you realize what nonsense you have uttered? How can 'you', or anyone else, *have* consciousness? Do you realize the unimaginable greatness, the holiness of what you so casually call 'consciousness'? Give it whatever name you like, the word is not what it means. How can you ever forget the basic truth that *consciousness is the very expression of what-we-are.* It is through the stirring of consciousness that the unmanifest Absolute becomes aware of its awareness through manifestation, and the whole universe comes into existence.

It may be through inadvertence that you used these words, I don't know, but the very inadvertence displays the strength of the conditioning which makes you identify yourself with the body. You think you are the body and that the body has the consciousness. If you must consider the matter in terms of one possessing the other, surely it is consciousness that is in possession of not only the body that you think you are but the millions of other bodies through which consciousness functions as Prajnā.

*   *   *

Friday, 17 July 1981 — It was the sacred day of Gurū Pūrnimā and Maharaj must have drawn heavily on his dwindling physical resources, to say a few words on this most auspicious day. He was sitting up in bed, with a thick pullover on, inspite of the small room being quite warm due to over-crowding of devotees. He started talking very feebly, but soon his voice seemed to gather a new strength.

You people have been coming here hoping all the time that I would give you a programme of what you should *do* in order to get 'liberation.' And what I keep telling you is that since there is no entity as such, the question of bondage does not arise; and that if one is not bound there is no need for liberation. All I can do is to show you that *what you are is not what you think you are.*

But what I say is not acceptable to most of you. And some of you go elsewhere, where they are happy to be given a list of *do's* and *dont's.* What is more, they act on such instructions with faith and diligence. But what they do not realize is that whatever they practise as an 'entity only strengthens their identification with the illusory entity and, therefore, understanding of the Truth remains as far away as ever.

People imagine that they must somehow change themselves from imperfect human beings into perfect human beings known as sages. If only they would see the absurdity in this thinking. The one who is thinking along these lines is himself only a concept, an appearance, a character in a dream. How can a mere phenomenal phantom awaken from a dream by perfecting itself?

The only 'awakening' is *apperceiving of that-which-is*. Indeed there is no question of a 'who' in this apperceiving because the apperceiving itself is one's true nature; and the pre-requisite of such apperceiving is the disappearance of the phenomenon. *What is apperceived is manifestation as a whole*, not by a 'who' keeping himself as a separate observer. The apperceiving is the total functioning of the Absolute — *apperceiving is what you are*. The universe appearing in consciousness is a mirror which reflects every sentient being, i.e. consciousness is the very source of the apparent universe. Consciousness is not different from its manifested content.

And such apperceiving has nothing whatever to do with a 'who', with a phenomenon, an appearance in consciousness which is only an infinitesimal part of the total functioning. The profound intuitive understanding of this fact is the only 'awakening', or 'enlightenment', the only illusory 'liberation' from an illusory 'bondage', the awakening from the living-dream.

What does the Guru do? A self-realized Guru would do the only thing that could be done; point a finger towards the Sadguru that is within. The Sadguru is always there whether you remember him or not, but a constant association with him — irrespective of whatever you may be doing — is all that is necessary. Anything else by way of effort will not only not help, but would be a hindrance and a hazard.

*   *   *

Sunday, 26 July 1981 — There was the usual Sunday morning crowd. The room was filled to capacity. Maharaj smiled and said that inspite of knowing that he was not in a position to speak people continued to visit him. What did

they expect to get? With considerable effort, and support
from his attendant devotee, he sat up. He looked around and
said that he was not able to recognize people, but if there
were any questions, let them not be kept bottled up. Do try,
however, he added, to keep in mind that at the intellectual
level there could be no end to questions.

One visitor asked: During the course of the search for
one's true nature, the world without and the mind within
create numerous obstructions. Why? And what should one
do? Maharaj quickly answered: Hang on to the one who is
searching. That is all you need do, and indeed, there is
nothing else you could really do. If you do this — i.e. never
leaving the one-in-search to escape you — you will
ultimately find that the seeker is none other than
consciousness seeking its source, and that the *seeker himself*
is both the seeking and the sought, and that is you.

There were several other questions which Maharaj
disposed of more or less summarily, as they related to one's
behaviour in the world, his main point being that it is nature,
or consciousness in action, which was responsible for the
spontaneous growth of the body from the moment of
conception to the birth of the body and further on from
infancy and childhood through youth to full development
and finally to decay. "Why do you suddenly accept
responsibility, for the actions of the body, and thereby the
bondage of retribution for such actions?" he asked.

Finally, towards the end, came the question: 'Is there any
difference' between a person who is an Avadhūta and
another who is a Jnānī?" I am asking the question because I
want to know how a self-realized person acts in this world.'

Maharaj laughed, and said: All your words as questions
and all my words as answers seem to go the same way into
nothingness. Had even a single answer of mine found its
mark, there would not be any more questions. So, in a way,
what happens is best; your continued questions and my
answers both contribute towards some entertainment to pass
the time! Indeed, there is nothing else to be done since there
is no 'purpose' to this that is seen as the Universe — it is all

Līlā, and we join in it. But we must understand this.

However, let us deal with your question. Avadhūta, Jnānī, self-realized are all names of a state, the very basic assumption of which is the total negation of the separateness of an individual entity, and yet the question is based on an understanding that a Jnānī is a 'person', and you want to know how such a person acts in this world. Do you see the contradiction in terms? As soon as there is self-realization, the difference between a self and the others disappears, and, of course, along with it the doership of the pseudo-personality. Therefore, once self-realization happens — do understand that 'one' does not 'acquire' self-realization — the sense of volition, or desire, or choice of action cannot remain.

Do try to understand the significance of what I have just said. If you have understood it, you will also have understood that *there can be no self-realized 'person'* and, therefore, there is no question of how a self-realized person acts in the world. What happens to the body? The response to external situations is spontaneous, intuitional, without the interference of the individual divided mind, and thus excludes any question of volitional activity.

*   *   *

Saturday, 8 August 1981 — A young lady asked Maharaj about the significance and usefulness of repeating a Japa. Maharaj said that he would interpret the word 'Japa' in its meaning as the 'purposive' noun, which would be 'protecting'.

He continued: By continuously repeating a Japa, or a Mantra, either as one word or a combination of words, you intend to 'protect' something. What does one want to protect? Something that one 'loves' most. What does one love most? Something which one 'needs' most: And what is it that one needs most? Something without which nothing else has any meaning, any value. Is it not the 'animus', the sense of animating presence, the consciousness, without which you cannot know anything or enjoy anything? This most precious 'need' is consciousness which you want to 'protect' at any cost, and the best way to protect anything is not to be away from it at all. Is it not?

So, the main purpose of repeating a Japa continuously is to remain one with consciousness all the time. But you must understand that this 'practice' will enable you to achieve your 'purpose' only for the limited duration while you repeat the Japa. A clear apperception of your true nature, on the other hand, is not at all based on the concept of time; apperception is intemporality.

*   *   *

Sunday, 9 August 1981 — The same young lady wanted to know whether the practice of observing a day every week as the 'day of silence' was a good one. Maharaj smiled and said that it would be an excellent practice if the significance of the word 'silence' was clearly understood. Maharaj explained: I have heard of certain Mahātmās and Gurūs, greatly interested in politics, observing 'days of silence', when they do not speak but communicate with the aid of pen and paper. I am sure their throats get a lot of much-needed rest, but other than that, I doubt if there could be any other benefit.

What I would understand by *'silence' is total absence of word and thought.* Have you ever considered from where the word comes? Before a word becomes vocal, it has to be a thought; a movement in consciousness, and therefore, the source of the word as well as the thought is consciousness. Once you understand this, you will also understand that perfect silence can only be in the absence of thought — only when thought ceases, and conceptualization and objectivization are also suspended. When conceptualization ceases, identity, which is the basis of conceptualization, cannot remain, and in the absence of identity there is no bondage.

*   *   *

Tuesday, 18 August 1981 — This morning Maharaj was too weak to speak. The suggestion that one of the recorded tapes of his talks be played was approved by him. After about twenty minutes of this, he asked that the tape be stopped. He sat up in his bed with some difficulty, and whispered a message: "Think on what you have heard just now — what you heard and, infinitely more important, who heard it".

After this brief whispered message words failed the Master. His throat got choked. He closed his eyes, his frail physical resources grappling with an excruciating pain. And we watched helplessly.   ●●

57

The Last Moments: Mahāsamādhī

Tuesday, 8 September 1981 — Sri Nisargadatta Maharaj today attained Mahāsamādhī at 7.32 p.m. at his residence Ashram.

When I arrived in the morning at his residence as usual, a little before 10 a.m. I thought Maharaj appeared considerably better than he was the previous day. His face had better colour and his eyes were more alert, but I gathered from his son that the doctor had observed that, as his chest was heavily congested and administration of oxygen was necessary. An oxygen cylinder had been arranged.

By the time I left at about 11 a.m. Maharaj had accepted first a cup of milk and a little later a cup of tea, and it appeared that he was feeling more comfortable. But when my friend Mullarpattan and I were leaving together, Mullarpattan told Maharaj that he would come again later in the afternoon as usual. Maharaj knew that generally I visited him only in the mornings, but today he specifically asked me when I would come again. I was a little startled at this question but, sensing his intent, I said I would drop in again in the evening and he seemed pleased. As we were leaving Maharaj said that he was feeling sleepy and would rest awhile.

I had a visitor in the afternoon. He stayed on a bit longer than I had expected. At about 6.30 p.m. as I was about to leave for Maharaj's residence, there was a telephone call from Mullarpattan to say that Maharaj's condition was causing serious anxiety. I rushed to Maharaj's residence and found oxygen being administered. His eyes were open, but with a blank expression which indicated that he was perhaps in the no-mind state. His breathing was laboured and it seemed that the end could not be far away.

His breathing, which was getting shallower and shallower, finally stopped altogether at 7.32 p.m. Maharaj had made the transition from the relative to the Absolute with the greatest ease and peace. Mullarpattan and I were there when the end came, along with the members of Maharaj's family and two of his personal attendants. It was decided that the funeral would take place the next day.

Wednesday, 9 September 1981 — Maharaj's body was placed in a reclining position in the special medical chair which a Belgian devotee, Josef Nauwelaerts, had personally brought over to Bombay only five weeks ago. Then we proceeded to the Banganga cremation ground in a procession which comprised several hundred devotees. The Samādhī of Maharaj's Guru, Sri Sidharamshwar Maharaj, is located on these grounds.

The funeral procession started at about 12.15 p.m. Maharaj's body was carried in a truck profusely decorated with flowers and, apart from the hundreds who joined the procession on his last journey, many others paid their respects to him along the way. We reached the cremation ground at 2.45 p.m.

The funeral pyre was lit by Maharaj's son at 3.40 p.m. at the end of a simple but moving ceremony, which started with the usual Āratī before Maharaj's Guru's shrine, as this was his practice before starting on a journey.

The physical form of the Master got merged into the elements of which it was made. Saying anything further about the Master would be both superfluous and inadequate, and wholly against Maharaj's teaching. Truth must be apperceived; it becomes a concept when given expression to.   ⚬●

The Core of the Teaching

The core of Śri Nisargadatta Maharaj's teaching is the knowledge of one's own true identity. This knowledge is indeed the pivotal point around which moves everything. It is the crucial truth. And the apperception of this truth arises only from intense personal experience, not from a study of religious texts, which, according to Maharaj, are nothing but 'hearsay'. Taking his stand on the bedrock of incontrovertible facts and totally discarding all assumptions and speculations, he often addresses a new visitor in the following words:

"You are sitting there, I am sitting here, and there is the world outside — and, for the moment, we may assume that there must be a creator, let us say God. These three/four items are facts or experience, not 'hearsay'. Let us confine our conversation to these items only." This basis automatically excludes along with the 'hearsay' the traditional texts too, and therefore there is always an exhilarating sense of freshness and freedom to Maharaj's talks. His words need no support from someone else's words or experiences which, after all, is all that the traditional texts can mean. This approach completely disarms those 'educated' people who come to impress the other visitors with their learning, and at the same time hope to get a certificate from Maharaj about their own highly evolved state. At the same time it greatly encourages the genuine seeker who would prefer to start from scratch.

On this basis a visitor usually finds himself without too many questions because all his pre-planned questions generally happen to be based on 'hearsay'. Maharaj usually helps such a visitor by prompting a query such as: What is it without which no one would be able to perceive anything or do anything? Without which you would not be able to ask any questions and I would not be able to answer? If you and I were not conscious, could we have had this conversation? What is 'consciousness'? Is it not the sense of being present, being alive? This sense of Conscious Presence does not really have reference to any individual being present: It is sense of conscious presence, as such. Without this consciousness, when, for instance, consciousness leaves the body at death, the body is quickly discarded — buried or cremated — because otherwise in no time the putrefied flesh would start stinking. Where, then, is the individual who, when consciousness was there, might have been considered a genius? He is said to have 'died'.

Consciousness — the Basis of all Manifestation

Maharaj tells the visitors that it is only about this consciousness or *I-am-ness* that he always talks. Any enquiries about anything else would be useless because this consciousness must be there before anything else can *be*. If I am not (conscious), he says, the world is not (as in deep sleep). It is only when I am conscious that the world exists for me. All inquiries of the seeker, Maharaj asserts, must therefore relate to this consciousness: How did it arise? What is its source? What sustains it? What is its nature? The answers to these queries lead to true knowledge. Without consciousness there can be no phenomenal existence, and therefore consciousness is the highest God that an individual in his individuality can conceive, although he may give it any name — Krishna, Ishwara, Shiva, Christ etc. When consciousness leaves the body, there is no individual, no world, no God.

The relationship between the physical body and consciousness, says Maharaj, must be very clearly perceived. Consciousness can be conscious of itself only so long as it has manifested itself in a phenomenal form, a body, whether it is that of an insect, or a worm, or an animal, or a human being.

Without the body, in unmanifested state, consciousness is not conscious of itself. Without consciousness the body is merely dead material. The body, therefore, says Maharaj, is the food that sustains consciousness and the instrument through which consciousness functions. In fact, he says, consciousness is the 'nature', or 'suchness', or 'taste' of the physical body like sweetness is of sugar.

After we have understood this intimate relation between the body and consciousness, Maharaj asks us to find out the source of this body-consciousness. How did it come about? The source of the human body is the male sperm fertilized in the ovum of a female womb, and when conception takes place, consciousness is latent therein. It is this — the fertilized male sperm with consciousness latent in it — that grows in the mother's womb, is delivered in due course as a baby, grows into infancy and thereafter through its span of life. What is the force behind this natural growth? Nothing other than consciousness which is latent in the male sperm, the latter itself being the essence of the food consumed by the parents. It should be clear then, says Maharaj, that consciousness is the very nature of the physical body (like sweetness of sugar) and that the physical body is made of and sustained by food, which is the essence of the five elements. In this spontaneous natural process, the individual, as such, does not have any significance. The individual body is made of food, and consciousness is universal, all-pervading. How can the individual claim either separate existence, or bondage and liberation for himself?

Has any individual been consulted about his 'birth' as the issue of particular parents? The 'me' and 'mine' have come about only after the birth, which is clearly the result of a natural process in which neither the parents nor the baby has any choice. In other words, Maharaj points out, the body-cum-consciousness is a phenomenal unit which has spontaneously been created out of the five elements (space, air, fire, water, and earth) and the three attributes (Sattva, Rajas and Tamas). This unit grows during its life-span and then 'dies' — that is, goes back to the five elements, and consciousness that was limited by the body is released into Impersonal Consciousness.

Now, asks Maharaj, in this natural process of the creation and destruction of a phenomenal unit, where is the question of a 'you'? You have never been a party to the creation of the phenomenal unit that 'you' are supposed to be. You have been told by your parents that you were 'born' and that a particular body is 'you'. You really have no actual experience of being born. What is born is a phenomenal unit, a psychosomatic apparatus that is activated by consciousness. If consciousness is not there, the body-apparatus is not only useless but has to be disposed of as quickly as possible.

Who then are *you?* You are, says Maharaj, what you were before the body-cum-consciousness came into being, what you were 'a hundred years ago'!

The question that naturally arises at this stage is: Who then acts in the ·world as the body? The answer according to Maharaj is that in manifestation consciousness is every-thing. It is consciousness that acts through the millions of bodies according to the innate character of the composition of each body. There are millions of psychosomatic forms but no two forms are exactly alike in all respects because each form has a distinctive combination of the five elements plus the three attributes. Each element has its own characteristics and so has each attribute. Imagine the millions of gradations that each of these eight aspects can have, and the resulting billions and trillions of permutations and combinations that can be effected! Consciousness acts through the physical bodies, each of which has its own temperament and charac-ter, based partly on its physical composition and partly on the conditioning it has received. If this is clearly perceived it should be also crystal clear that no individual has the au-tonomy to act independently. But the individual, in his ig-norance, believes that it is he who acts; he 'takes delivery', says Maharaj, of the actions that take place, binds himself in illusory bondage, and suffers pain and pleasure. This is how 'bondage' arises.

Maharaj wants us to be clear on one point: Man considers

himself a special being, apart from all other creation. But so far as the ingredients of the physical construct are concerned, there is no difference between the various kinds of sentient creatures. Only the process of creation differs.

The Essential Purpose of Paramārtha

Maharaj constantly urges us not to miss, forget, overlook, or ignore the essential purpose of all Paramārtha i.e. the ultimate understanding, and to know our Svarūpa i.e. our true identity. What is our true identity? Maharaj would say: Unmanifested, in stillness, our identity is the Absolute Unicity — Pure Awareness not aware of itself; manifested, functioning in duality, our identity is consciousness seeking itself as the 'other' because 'it cannot tolerate its own presence.' In other words, says Maharaj, on our original state of the timeless, changeless, Absolute Noumenality, the body-cum-consciousness has appeared like a temporary illness, without cause or reason, as part of the total 'functioning' of the Impersonal Consciousness in its role as Prajnā. Each phenomenal form works out its allotted duration and at the end of its life-span disappears as spontaneously as it appeared, and consciousness, relieved of its physical limitation, no longer conscious of itself, merges in Awareness: one is neither born nor does one die. Consciousness in order to manifest itself needs physical forms for its functioning and is constantly creating new forms and destroying old forms.

If this is the natural process of the total functioning of consciousness, the question arises: How does the individual entity and its bondage come into existence? A brief answer, says Maharaj, would be to say that consciousness, limited by the confines of the physical form and not finding any other support, deludes itself into an identification with the particular body and thus creates a pseudo-entity; and this pseudo-entity, mistaking itself as the doer of the actions (which actually form part of the total spontaneous functioning of Prajnā) must accept the consequences and thereby subject itself to the bondage of the cause and effect of the Karma idea.

The Question of Re-birth

Maharaj rejects the idea of re-birth or re-incarnation out of hand, and the basis for such rejection is so simple that it humbles us: *the entity which is supposed to be re-born does not exist,* except as a mere concept! How can a concept be re-born?

Maharaj in all innocence asks the protagonist of re-birth: "Please, I want to know, who is it that would be re-born?" The body 'dies' and, after death, is demolished — buried or cremated — as quickly as possible. The body, in other words, has been irreparably, irretrievably, irrevocably destroyed. That body, therefore, which was an objective thing cannot be re-born. How then can anything non-objective like the life-force (the breath), which, on the death of the body, merged with the air outside, or the consciousness which merged with the Impersonal Consciousness, be re-born either?

Perhaps, says Maharaj, you will say that the entity concerned will be re-born. But that would be utterly ridiculous. You do know that the 'entity' is nothing but a concept, a hallucination which arises when consciousness mistakenly identifies itself with the particular form.

How did the idea of re-birth arise at all? It was perhaps conceived as some sort of an acceptable working theory to satisfy the simpler people who were not intelligent enough to think beyond the parameters of the manifested world.

The Pseudo-entity

However, in order to see clearly how the pseudo-entity, or the ego (who is supposed to be the cause and the object of supposed bondage) arises, it is necessary to understand the conceptual process for manifestation. What we are Absolutely, noumenally, is unicity-absolute-subjectivity without the slightest touch of objectivity. The only way *this-that-we-are* can manifest itself is through a process of duality, the start of which is the stirring of consciousness, the sense of 'I am'. This process of manifestation-objectivization, which was so far totally absent, entails a dichotomy into a subject that perceives and an object that is perceived; cognizer and the cognized.

The noumenon — pure subjectivity — must always remain the only subject. Therefore, the supposed cognizer and the supposed cognized are both objects in consciousness. This is the essential factor to be borne in mind. It is only in consciousness that this process can occur. Every imaginable thing — every kind of phenomenon — that our senses perceive and our mind interprets is an appearance in our consciousness. Each of us exists only as an object, an appearance in someone else's consciousness. The cognizer and the cognized are both objects in consciousness but (and this is the important point regarding the pseudo-entity) that which cognizes the object assumes that it is the subject of the cognition for other objects, in a world external to itself, and this cognizing subject regards its pseudo-subjectivity as constituting an independent, autonomous entity — a 'self' — with the power of volitional action!

The principle of duality, which starts with the sense 'I am', and on which is based the entire phenomenal manifestation, is carried a step further when the pseudo-entity, in its role as the pseudo-subject, begins the process of reasoning by comparing inter-dependent and opposing counterparts (such as good and bad, pure and impure, merit and sin, presence and absence, great and small etc.), and, after the comparison, discriminating between them. This constitutes the process of conceptualization.

Apart from this dichotomy of subject and object, the process of phenomenal manifestation depends on the basic concept of space and time. In the absence of the concept of 'space', no object could become apparent with its three-dimensional volume; similarly, in the absence of the related concept of 'time', the three-dimensional object could not be perceived — nor any movement measured — without the duration necessary to make the object perceivable. The process of phenomenal manifestation, therefore, takes place in conceptual space-time, in which the objects become appearances in consciousness, perceived and cognized by consciousness, through a process of conceptualization the basis of which is a splitting into the perceiving pseudo-subject and the perceived object. The result of the identification with the cognizer element in the process of manifestation is the conception of the pseudo-personality with personal choice of action. And this is the whole basis of the illusory 'bondage'.

Understand the whole process of phenomenal manifestation, says Maharaj, not in bits and pieces but in one flash of apperception. The Absolute, the noumenon is the unmanifested aspect and the phenomenon, the manifested aspect of what we are. *They are not different.* A crude simile would be the substance and its shadow, except that the manifested would be the shadow of the formless unmanifested! The Absolute noumenon is intemporal, spaceless, not perceptible to the senses; the phenomena are time-bound, with a limited form and perceptible to the senses. *Noumenon is what we are; phenomena are what we appear to be* as separate objects in consciousness. Identification of the unicity (or the subject) that we *are*, with the separateness in duality (or the object) that we *appear to be*, constitutes 'bondage' and disidentification (from this identification) constitutes 'liberation'. But both 'bondage' and 'liberation' are illusory because there is no such entity who is in bondage, wanting liberation; the entity is only a concept arising out of the identification of consciousness with an apparent object that is merely an appearance in consciousness!

Life a Living-dream

Once this is clearly apperceived, it cannot but be understood that our idea of 'living our lives' is a joke because the idea of living our lives is based on the wrong belief that what we do are all acts of our volition. Who can exercise this volition when we have just apperceived that there is no entity to exercise it? 'Living' as such is really nothing other than the functioning of consciousness through the millions of physical forms, but mistaken for an individual life.

Maharaj also explains that this basic apperception comports the understanding that life is only a living-dream. At this stage, it should be clear that whatever one sees, hears, tastes, smells or touches is sensorially perceived and that this perception is in fact merely a cognition in consciousness — indeed, that the entity whose senses perceived it is itself merely an appearance in the consciousness of the 'other' one who perceives this entity as an object! Thus, the objects perceived mistakenly as entities in the consciousness of one another not being autonomous entities, what really happens is that there is no perceiver as such, but only the perceiving of conceptual objects moving in conceptual space, in conceptual duration. Are all these not clearly the aspects of the dream which we experience while asleep? When the dreamer wakes up the dreaming ends, and the one who is awake is no longer concerned about the other 'entities' in the dream. Similarly, in the living-dream, the one who is awake (the one who realizes that nothing perceivable by the senses, including the 'entity' one thinks one is, can be anything other than a mere appearance in consciousness) is no longer concerned about the other dream figures in the living-dream. The awakened one realizes that he is the unconditioned Absolute Subjectivity on which the stirring of consciousness started this living-dream spontaneously, without cause or reason, and just 'lives' out the dream till, at the end of the allotted span, consciousness once again spontaneously merges in the Absolute Subjectivity.

Spiritual Practices: Volition

Having followed Maharaj thus far, the reaction from most visitors is astonishingly similar. The question is asked: What you have said is very profound and I think I understand it intellectually, but what is it exactly that one should *do* in order to actually experience it? Maharaj sometimes hides his utter frustration and at other times he flares up at this question, but his usual answer to the question is a counter-question: Who is this 'one' who thinks he must do something — and to achieve what? Once it is understood that an entity is merely an erroneous concept, that a body like any other phenomenon is merely an experience in consciousness, and that there is no one to exercise any volition, where is the question of anyone *doing* anything? Understanding — apperception — is all. To be thoroughly and totally impregnated by this apperception is all the 'doing' that is necessary for liberation; and no amount of 'doing' will achieve it without the total annihilation of the erroneous concept of an independent entity with autonomy of action. The 'I' cannot emerge without the annihilation of the 'me'. *When the 'me' disappears, you are I.*

If the arrow has hit the target, as Maharaj says, there could not possibly be any more questions. But direct and intuitive apperception of the facts — the flight of the arrow — is made difficult by the interference of conceptualization by the intellect. Intellectual understanding is based on cause and effect, one of the aspects of the temporal dualism on which conceptualization is based. Intuitional understanding — direct understanding — on the other hand, is intemporal where cause and effect are one. It is intellectual understanding that leads to the question: If there is no autonomous entity to exercise any volition, how is non-volitional living accomplished? Or, how is one supposed to live and act in the world?

When such a question is asked Maharaj's usual answer would be:"It doesn't matter what you do so long as you have truly understood what I am talking about. In another way, it also does not matter if you have not understood what I am talking about!" Obviously the point is that all our past experiences, if carefully analyzed, would clearly show that our lives, instead of being lived *by* us as we seem to think, are in fact being lived *for* us like all the characters in one's dream and that, therefore, volition is really not a significant factor in our lives. A little thought would show us what an infinitesimally small part of our total physical or organic functioning depends on our volition. Maharaj asks: How long can you live without sleep, without food or water? How long can you go along without the excretary movements of the body? How long can you remain without breathing? Do you have the absolute volition to remain alive even for the next five mi-

nutes? Did you exercise your volition when you were conceived? And when the conceived material grew in the
mother's womb?

When Maharaj tells us that it really does not matter what
we do, he obviously wants us to comprehend that there
cannot be any entity to exercise any effective volition —
either doing or not doing — that what we take to be the
result of our volition is only the inevitable. When it corres-
ponds with what we consider to be agreeable to us at the
time, we take pride in our 'volitional action' and consider it a
personal achievement, and when it is not, it becomes a
matter of anger, unhappiness and frustration for us. Indeed,
says Maharaj, accepting the doership on the basis of volition
of something that is part of the total functioning of consciousness is the chain that binds the phenomenal individual in apparent 'bondage' — apparent because there is no
entity to be bound — and the realization of the very absurdity of the pseudo-subject trying to act independently of the
Prajñā-ic functioning is the 'awakening'. Only such realization can lead to a perfect acceptance with equanimity of
whatever events may occur until the duration of the life span
is over, and, while life is thus being lived, there would
obviously be a definite sense of an all-enveloping unity
because the 'others' would be perceived not as objects of a
pseudo-subject but as the manifested aspects of the same
noumenal subjectivity that one *is*. In other words, living
would be free living, where neither the positive doing nor
the negative non-doing of a pseudo-entity would prevail,
since, in the absence of any intentions, there is no volition.
Without conceptual intentions, all actions would be spontaneous; the actor playing his part in this life-play or living
one's living-dream taking life as it comes. Once there is
apperception of *that-which-is*, says Maharaj, all life becomes what it has always been — Līlā, an 'entertainment'.

When asked what he would do in a given set of circumstances, Maharaj has answered in absolute innocence: "I do
not know." This is exactly correct because, in what might
seem to be identical circumstances, on different occasions

his actions might be unpredictable, but on each occasion the action would be spontaneous! Maharaj often says that whatever is spontaneous is correct because, in the absence of conceptualizing, the spontaneous is natural and therefore correct without any reasoning, comparison or any cause-effect.

Listening to the words of the Gurū gets top priority from Maharaj. He says that the quickest way towards self-realization (although he makes it amply clear that there is really no 'way' and no 'one' to go anywhere) is listening (Shravana), reflecting (Manana) and meditating thereon (Nididhyāsana). Even these words, Maharaj urges repeatedly, have to be used merely for communicating, and once the intention and meaning is grasped, the words — all words — must be thrown away in order to prevent intellect from raising conceptual structures thereon.

Maharaj repeatedly asserts that his words are not addressed to any individual entity but to consciousness. Words arise from consciousness and are addressed to consciousness. It is consciousness which should listen to the words, and after the meaning is intuitively grasped, the words should be allowed to merge in consciousness. If the listening is done by 'an individual' with the intention of getting some benefit with the aid of the intellect, Maharaj warns, all would be lost. Indeed, it is exactly the interference of the intellect that should be avoided. As has been made clear earlier, it is the emptiness of the pseudo-entity that must be apperceived. So long as it is an entity that is listening to words, how can the words achieve even the limited purpose of pointing in the right direction, the right direction being away from phenomenality which is the source of both the entity and the words themselves! Words can throw up their deep and subtle meaning only if they are accepted intuitively without the interpretative interference of the intellect; otherwise the result would be a mere intellectual understanding of the world 'outside' by an entity that keeps itself separate from what it understands to be illusory. You cannot, says Maharaj, take out a tiny bit of the total pheno-

menal manifestation as your separate self and at the same
time understand *that-which-is. It is only in the total annihi-*
lation of the pseudo-entity that true apperception can take
place.

The Magnificent Fraud

Consciousness, says Maharaj, is the beguiling, bewitching
Mahāmāyā, the most magnificent fraud ever! This enchanting sense of presence is only a sense, a concept which comes
upon the Unmanifest Absolute like an unwelcome guest who
takes over the household so insidiously that the host is lulled
into a sense of false security and well-being. Maharaj also
calls it 'a temporary illness' that produces delirium during its
currency!

This sense of being alive — being present — is so intoxi-
cating that one is enchanted by the manifestation that it
presents. One gets so involved in the spectacle that one
rarely cares to find out if the spectacle really exists or is
merely a vision, a hallucination, a dream, a mirage. One sees
the tree and is so enchanted by it that one forgets that the tree
is nothing other than the growth of the seed which is the true
source of it. The aim of Paramārtha (Parama-artha, the core
meaning) is to seek the source, the seed. What is the seed of
this manifestation? If you are not conscious, asks Maharaj, is
there any manifestation at all of any kind? If you are not
conscious, does the universe exist for you? *It is only when*
you are (conscious) *that the world is.* So, obviously the
universe is contained in the speck of consciousness (that is
supposed to exist in the tiniest aperture in the centre of the
skull). Consciousness cannot manifest itself, cannot be conscious of itself, unless there is a psychosomatic apparatus,
the body. What is the source of the body? Obviously the male
sperm fertilized in an ovum of the womb of a female. What is
the source of the sperm and the ovum? The food consumed
by the parents. Now, asks Maharaj, what is the conclusion we
arrive at? The Absolute, the ultimate potential, the source of
everything could *not* possibly be so mundane as 'food'!
Therefore, this I-am-ness, the consciousness, this sense of
presence cannot be anything but a concept, a vision, a

dream, a hallucination! And this consciousness is the source of all manifestation — indeed it *is* manifestation!

There is a basic fundamental question at this stage. Who has come to this conclusion? Who else can it be but 'I'? 'I' who am responsible for every kind of manifestation, I who *am* every kind of manifested phenomenon, I who was present a hundred years ago, I who was present before 'time' was conceived, I who am intemporality, I who am awareness not aware of itself because in that, my true state of Wholeness, Unicity, there is neither presence nor absence; *absence of the presence of presence, absence of the presence of absence is what-I-am* (And every sentient being can say this — not as himself but as 'I').

Do we need it all again, briefly? Here it is:

(1) Manifested existence is phenomenal, and phenomena being appearance sensorially cognizable and time-bound is a vision, a dream, a hallucination and therefore untrue. Unmanifested existence is Absolute, intemporal, spaceless, not aware of existing, sensorially not cognizable, eternal, therefore true. Who says this? Consciousness, of course, trying to cognize itself and not succeeding because *cognizing* (there is no cognizer as such) cannot cognize that which itself is cognizing: An eye can not see itself although it sees everything else. *The seeker is the sought*: This is the basic all-important *truth*.

(2) I, unmanifested, am the total potentiality, the absolute absence of the known and the knowable, the absolute presence of the unknown and the unknowable. I, manifest, am the totality of all phenomena, totality of the known in the inconceivability of the unmanifested unknown.

(3) There can be only I — the eternal I — totally unconditioned, without the slightest touch of any attribute, pure subjectivity. *The mere thought of 'me' is immediate and spontaneous (but illusory) bondage:* Let the *me* disappear and, immediately and spontaneously, *you are I*.

(4) Phenomenally, 'me' (and 'you' and 'he') is only an appearance in consciousness: How can an appearance be in bondage? Noumenally, how can I — pure subjectivity —

need any liberation? Liberation is only being rid of the idea that there is any 'one' who needs liberation.

(5) How is one to know if one is making 'progress' spiritually? Could it be that the surest sign of 'progress' is a lack of concern about progress and an absence of anxiety about liberation in the wake of clear apprehension? An instant apperception of the total 'functioning' of Nisarga (nature) in which there is no place for an autonomous entity.   ••

A Note on Consciousness

It would perhaps be a truism to say that any kind of confusion regarding the concept of consciousness arises because, and only because the essential nature of consciousness has not been apprehended. But it is necessary to say so. This confusion is somewhat comparable to the classic case of the confusion created in the minds of the group of blind men when each of them touched and felt only one part of the elephant and decided what the elephant was like.

In trying to get a clear idea of what Maharaj intends to convey by the word 'consciousness', it would help us if at the very outset we would bear in mind the basic fact that in the absence of consciousness there cannot be existence of any kind, and consciousness itself is merely the thought — *I am*. Therefore whatever arises in consciousness — and appears as a thing, an object, or an event or a feeling — can also only be of the nature of thought, i.e. without existence on its own. This means in effect that man himself, being only an appearance in the consciousness of another, can have no substance as such. Maharaj sets the whole problem in perspective by saying that the entire manifested universe is 'like the child of a barren woman' — an illusion. All further elucidation of the problem must therefore be considered in this perspective.

In deep sleep, when consciousness is resting and the mind is utterly still, there is no question of the existence either of the individual concerned or of other individuals and objects comprising the 'world'. In deep sleep one does not undergo any experience, either of pain or of pleasure, because any experience can arise only as a movement in consciousness.

One's miseries arise only when deep sleep is over and consciousness stirs either into dreams or into full wakefulness. It is from this point of view that Maharaj talks of consciousness as being 'the culprit': man suffers any experience only when there is the sense of conscious presence.

Awareness, Consciousness, the 'Individual'

'Awareness' is the name given to that state of absolute perfection when consciousness is at total rest and is not aware of its own *beingness*. (Whatever words are used to indicate *it*, they can only be a concept because in that state *it* cannot perceive itself.)

Consciousness becomes conscious of itself only when it begins to stir, and the thought, *I am*, arises. Why does consciousness arise at all? For no apparent reason other than it is its nature — like the wave on an expanse of water: 'the causeless cause', says Maharaj. Simultaneously, along with the primal thought *I am*, springs into existence the entire manifested universe in a split-second. When consciousness, which is impersonal in rest, manifests itself by objectifying itself as phenomena, it identifies itself with each sentient object and thus arises the concept of a separable personal individual 'I' which treats all other phenomena as its objects, and each sentient being becomes the subject vis-a-vis all other sentient objects, although all are really objects appearing in consciousness.

What constitutes 'bondage' is precisely this limiting of the pure subjectivity and the unlimited potential of the Absolute into a single insignificant object calling itself 'me', as separate from others. It is this phenomenal object, a mere appearance in the consciousness of others, who comes to Maharaj for 'liberation', and it is to this individual that Maharaj tells, *inter alia,* that the only one who can help him is consciousness, which is the only 'capital' every sentient being is born with, the only link he has with the Absolute. Consciousness is the 'culprit' that has brought man the illusory bondage and it is only consciousness that can help him to attain the illusory liberation. Consciousness is the Māyā, says Maharaj, that produces the illusory bondage, and it is also consciousness, the Īshvara, that acts as the Sadgurū and, if duly propitiated, unfolds the secret of the universe and provides the illusory liberation in this play of the living-dream in which consciousness is the only actor enacting all the multifareous roles. Therefore, says Maharaj, there is no power on earth that is greater than this consciousness, this sense of presence — *I am*, to which the illusory individual must direct all his prayers; and then this very consciousness will provide the illusory liberation for the illusory bondage of the illusory individual by revealing its true nature — which is none other than the seeker himself, but not as an individual!

The Nature of Consciousness and Manifestation

When Maharaj asks us to consider consciousness as the highest God and pray to it for guidance, he assumes, of course, that we still identify ourselves with our bodies and consider ourselves as separate entities with independent choice of action. But on this basis of individuality and freedom of choice, the manifested universe cannot yield its secret. Therefore, says Maharaj, pray with sincerity and ardour to consciousness, the source of all sentience, so that this hold of entity-fication will gradually loosen itself and enable the purified psyche to receive the secret of its true nature from consciousness, the Sadgurū.

The attachment of the human being to the body as a separate entity is due entirely to the conditioning he receives from the parents, elders and others, from the earliest moments of understanding, that he is the particular body with a particular name. Very soon he is convinced beyond any doubt that he is the body that is endowed both with the life-force of breath, inhaling and exhaling continuously, and with consciousness or sentience which comes and goes with the waking and sleeping states. Actually, all that has happened is that the noumenon has objectified itself into millions of forms (including the human forms) as phenomena constituting the total manifestation and its functioning, and these phenomenal objects are continuously created and destroyed in the process of manifestation, and none has any choice of action. Indeed, therefore, instead of the various human beings each possessing consciousness, it is Consciousness which possesses the millions of forms through which the noumenon can objectify itself. If there is clear understanding and deep conviction about this process of the continuous appearance and disappearance of manifestation, as in the case of the Jnānī, consciousness is then seen in a totally different light. THEN, consciousness in action i.e. the phenomena, are seen as the perishable instruments for manifestation to take place, although, of course, the manifestation is not different from the noumenon but only the objective aspect of the noumenon, the only subject.

This brings us to the point why Maharaj calls consciousness 'time-bound'. The answer is that Consciousness needs a physical form to manifest itself in, and the manifested consciousness *in that form* can last only so long as the physical form lasts. The physical form is made of and sustained and nourished by food, which is only the essence of the five elements (the mix of the vital fluids of the parents which causes conception in the female womb is itself the essence of the food consumed by the parents). When the physical form 'dies', the breath leaves the body and mingles with the air outside, and consciousness leaves the body and merges with the unmanifested consciousness. Consciousness within the body is therefore limited for its manifestation in each case by the span of life which each physical form has been allotted, and, therefore, is time-bound.

What all this amounts to may be recapitulated as under:-

(a) The individual human being considers consciousness (note the absence of the capital 'C') as part of the equipment which he has within the body ever since he was born. At this stage, therefore Maharaj tells him that his very existence depends upon this consciousness within his body. If he had been born without this consciousness, 'he' would have been thrown out and destroyed like a piece of dirt. Therefore, says Maharaj, understand that this consciousness is the only 'source' which can help him to understand his true nature;

(b) Then, Maharaj startles him out of his complacancy

with which he considers consciousness as his personal property, by telling him that it is not he as an individual who owns consciousness, but that it is Consciousness (note the capital 'c') — the manifested objective aspect of the unmanifested Absolute — in which appears the entire universe, including the millions of human beings; that, therefore, he is only a tiny part of the total manifestation, the whole show being only an illusion;

(c) If this position is clearly understood, it would also be perceived that, so long as the body exists, we are not the perishable body, the psychosomatic apparatus for the manifestation to take place, but the animating consciousness which gives sentience to the physical apparatus. Once, however, the body 'dies', and the manifested consciousness leaves the body and merges with the unmanifest consciousness, *we are the Consciousness at rest — the Absolute Awareness.*

The Essential Identity

At this stage, the point that remains to be dealt with, in order to make this meditation reasonably complete in itself, is to bring out the essential identity of the non-manifest and the manifest, the noumenon and the phenomena, the Absolute and the relative, presence and absence, and indeed all the inter-related opposites or counterparts. All these sets represent the various aspects of the mind (mind being the content of consciousness) constituting the dualism which is the basis of all manifestation: the observer and the observed, the knower and the known. As Maharaj says, apperceiving the basic identity of the inter-related opposites means 'liberation' because then it will be realized that the seeker himself is the sought; that all distinctions only exist in duality, and that if the various inter-related opposites are superimposed on one another they would result in the annihilation of one another and thereby of the very condition of duality and thus bring about the fundamental unity.

It is perhaps necessary to repeat here that consciousness is manifestation and manifestation is in duality, but that this duality is created *within* the unicity of the unmanifested Absolute. The totality of the manifestation is not something projected by consciousness when it stirs into activity; the various objects constituting the manifestation have no substance or nature of their own other than consciousness which itself is the perceiving and the cognizing of the phenomena. The fact is that all manifestation, all phenomena, are appearances in consciousness, perceived by consciousness, and cognized by consciousness through the interpretation by the mind. If this fact is clearly perceived and understood, it will then be realized that consciousness is both the function-*ing* that takes place and also the perceive-*ing* of the functioning— and we (not the individuals but the eternal 'I') *are* that perceive-*ing*. Consciousness in action cannot be different from Consciousness at rest, the Absolute Awareness, which is the totality of all potential. In other words, the Consciousness-manifestation is the objective aspect of the subjective Awareness.

Once Consciousness stirs and the activity begins, the activity of manifestation and functioning can take place only in a state of apparent duality. 'Space' is the static aspect of the functioning concept: if there were no space, no phenomena with the three dimensional volume could be conceived. And 'time' (duration) is the active aspect of the functioning concept: if there were no duration, the conceived phenomena in space would not be perceivable. There can be neither manifestation nor functioning (neither human beings nor events) in the absence of the dual concept of space and time, known as 'space-time'; and these two aspects are separate only as a concept but lose their separateness when conceptualization ceases. In deep sleep, for instance, both space and time disappear and along with them all manifestation because duality can exist only in conceptualization. Let thought stop and all duality disappears.

Phenomena, in other words, cannot be conceived without noumenon, nor noumenon without phenomena. (The very idea of the noumenon is of course, within the area of the duality of conceptualization). When conceptualizing ceases, all duality comes to an end. When conceptualizing ceases there is neither phenomena nor noumenon because what remains is pure subjectivity— no experience of any kind and no one to demand any experience! To put all this briefly: all inter-related counterparts are inevitably separate only as concepts and essentially inseparable otherwise.

The Play of Unicity in Duality

If noumenon wishes to look at itself — we áre, of course, conceptualizing now — it cannot do so without objectivizing itself as phenomena. Noumenon, being pure subjectivity, cannot see itself as noumenon. The phenomenal manifestation, therefore, is not something from outside, 'projected' by the noumenon, but is an objectivization as manifestation *on* and *within* itself.

When, on the noumenon, consciousness stirs into being and there arises the sense of presence — I *am* — there springs up simultaneously the sense of duality the knower and the known, the experiencer and the.thing experienced. But the duality is only apparent and not real because the essential unicity cannot be dichotomized. The two aspects — Consciousness at rest (noumenality) and consciousness in action (phenomenality) — don't fall apart nor join each other because the dual aspect arises only as a concept. Shiva (noumenon) exists in the stirring of the Consciousness because such activity has no other source except Shiva; and the activity itself — the manifestation and the functioning (Shakti) — takes place on and within Shiva (noumenon). The duality is merely an illusion, a concept which does not and cannot affect the unicity of the Absolute. Do not forget that the conceptual creation of the universe is only 'the child of a barren woman'! If the duality were indeed real, each of the two parts would have had a nature of its own, different from that of the other. Therefore, the appearance and disappearance of the apparent duality are both an illusion which goes on continuously from moment to moment without any interval. The essential identity is innate.

Noumenon and phenomena (or any other words denoting

the relative conditions) are merely names which have to be used for communication in the dualistic state after manifestation takes place. They are merely two words used to describe the two states conceived in concept but they cannot disturb the basic unicity which remains totally unaffected. Waves may rise and subside but the expanse of water as such remains unaffected. The appearance and disappearance of manifested phenomena in Consciousness represent the play of Shiva (Līlā) in the traditional Indian viewpoint. Although for an analytical study Jnāna ánd Bhakti may be traditionally treated as separate, they are indeed two aspects of the same fundamental unity. This is why at the start of his famous treatise on Advaita philosophy 'Amritanubhava' (the Immortal Experience) the poet-saint of Maharashtra, Jnaneshvara Maharaj offers his obeisance 'with utmost humility' to this apparent duality of Shiva-Shakti so that they may divulge their true nature. (Here 'humility' obviously means not the opposite of 'pride' but the very negation of a separate entity who could be neither proud nor humble for the simple reason that true knowledge can come in only when there is total vacancy.)

Now we can understand why Maharaj calls 'consciousness' the highest God who should be propitiated with Bhakti and prayers so that it will divulge its true nature: time-bound in its relative conceptual aspect as far as the individual is concerned, but timeless and spaceless, and therefore, infinite and eternal when unconceived. A full realization of this true nature would annihilate the very seeker and merge him into the eternal peace of Consciousness at rest — the pure subjectivity, it. The entire manifestation and its functioning in consciousness — that we are in duality — is all a mere appearance, a Līlā, like the reflection of the sun in a dewdrop. The demolition of the reflection does not affect the sun. Consciousness in action is the time-bound 'Līlā' which at the end of its allotted period merges into the Consciousness at rest — infinite, unconditioned Awareness that is not aware of itself.   ••

Bhakti, Jnāna and the Individual

Some visitors to Maharaj, especially the foreign scholars among them, do not realize that he is not a 'learned' man in the usual sense of the word. They expect from him scholarly dissertations on various philosophical subjects. One such subject is the preference between Bhakti and Jnāna as a spiritual path. When asked such a question, Maharaj laughs and says how an almost illiterate man like himself could be expected to answer it. He might also point to someone in the audience and introduce him as a scholar with a master's degree in Indian philosophy, who was surely better qualified to enlighten the visitor. He would then, perhaps quietly, ask the visitor 'who' it is that wants this information and for what purpose. The visitor quickly looks at Maharaj to see if he was joking, but finds that he had asked the question in all seriousness: 'Who wants to know the answer?' And this question from Maharaj soon makes the visitor sense that his original query had lured him into deep waters which he had never charted before. Realizing his predicament, the Master would then make it easier for him by explaining that it is conceptualization which raises various such unnecessary issues, gets the individual trapped in its net and makes him forget the fundamental question as to 'who' is the questioner, really. Is the questioner the person he believes himself to be? Is there at all such a thing as a 'person', an individual entity, with independent choice of action to choose a particular spiritual path?

The main point in Maharaj's teaching is that in this living-dream of life we are not the dreamed characters, which we think we are, but that *we are the dreamer*, and it is our mistaken identification with the dreamed character, as a separate independent entity as the 'doer', that causes the illusion of 'bondage'. By the same token, then, it cannot be the dreamed character, a mere appearance, who can be 'awakened' or 'liberated'. Indeed, awakening lies in the dissolving of this 'appearance', and liberation consists in totally annihilating the false entity with which we have been mistakenly identifying ourselves. By the same token, furthermore, awakening or liberation cannot be 'achieved' by any efforts. Who will make the efforts — a phenomenon, a mere appearance? *Awakening can only happen*, and it can happen only when there is the utter conviction, through intuitive apperception, that we are the subjective dreamer and not the dreamed objects which disappear with the end of the dream. To take this theme to its logical conclusion, the final query would be: How does this intuitive apperception arise or happen? But then, that is exactly the point. If the process would be within the parameters of intellectual comprehension, how could it be an 'intuitive' one? Intellect is very much necessary to understand certain fundamentals, but there is a strict limit upto which intellect can go, and thereafter, it is only when intellect gives up all efforts and acknowledges total surrender that intuition takes over.

It should be clear therefore that the identification with an imaginary, independent, separate entity must totally disappear before there can be awakening or enlightenment or liberation. The mistaken identity must first be given up before the true identity can be assumed. What is false must go, before what is true can come in. This can happen, says Maharaj, in several ways. Deep intellectual concentration of the Jnāni on the source of the consciousness that we are can reach a point where duality, the basis of intellect, suddenly disappears and intuitive unicity takes over. Also, deep devotion of the Bhakta for his God can reach an intensity where, again, the duality between the Bhakta and his God suddenly disappears and there is realization that he the Bhakta and He the God are one, not two. The same result could follow through a long and arduous process of Yogic practice, or even through genuinely selfless social service. However, the final take-off point, in all cases, is the total annihilation of the mistaken individual identity. And at this final stage the miracle happens. The moment the false identity is liquidated, there is nothing left to identify with, except the totality! And this is the experience of the Jnānī, the Bhakta as well as the Yogī.

Maharaj hits the nail on the head in regard to this subject of devotion and knowledge when he says that the two are so inextricably blended together that they are in effect one and the same thing. Love for self and love for God are not different. The following words, reproduced from *I Am That* revised edition, chapter 46, page 213 are truly illuminating:

That which you are, your true self, you love it, and whatever you do, you do for your own happiness. To find it, to know it, to cherish it is your basic urge. Since time immemorial you loved yourself, but not wisely. Use your body and mind wisely in the service of the self, that is all. Be true to your own self, love your self absolutely. Do not pretend that you love others as yourself. Unless you have realized them as one with yourself, you cannot love them. Don't pretend to be what you are not, don't refuse to be what you are. Your love of others is the result of self-knowledge, not its cause. Without self-realization, no virtue is genuine. When you know beyond all doubting that the same life flows through all that is, and you are that life, you will love all naturally and spontaneously. When you realize the depth and fullness of your love for yourself, you know that every living being and the entire universe are included in your affection. But when you look at any thing as separate from you, you cannot love it for you are afraid of it. Alienation causes fear and fear deepens alienation. It is a vicious circle. Only self-realization can break it. Go for it resolutely.

The problem which Maharaj has set out so pointedly — that you cannot love anything which you consider as separate from you because then you are afraid of it, and the more you try the more difficult it becomes — is a type of problem which modern psychiatric anthropologists call the 'double-bind' type, where a person is required to do something contradictory. For example, the more you are asked to relax the more tense you become; the longer you want to hit the golf ball the more tense you become and the shorter the distance the ball travels!

A European visitor once told Maharaj: "The most important of the commandments is: 'Thou *shalt* love the Lord thy God'. But I find it most frustrating indeed, for this commandment is made difficult to obey by the addition of the words 'with *all* thy heart, and *all* thy soul, and *all* thy mind'. It is clearly meant that a mere hopefully pious act is not enough, since the added words emphasize that the love that is showed must not merely *appear* to be love, but must indeed *be* love. One may act *as if* one loved, but how was one to ensure that one did indeed *actually* love? How did one ensure spontaneity?" Maharaj's answer was simple and beautiful: Without self-realization no virtue is genuine; it is only when you arrive at the deepest conviction that the same life flows through everything, and that you are that life, that you begin to love all naturally and spontaneously. Such conviction, of course, can only come through an intuitive appreception, and Nature (Nisarga) will have its own course for this intuitive process.

In regard to the identity of the self and God, it is interesting to note the very close similarity of teaching between the great mystics of various faiths in different ages. We are told by St. John of the Cross, in his Canticles that "The thread of love binds so closely God and the soul, and so unites them, that it transforms them and makes them one by love; so that, though in essence different yet in glory and appearance the soul seems God, and God the soul." (Canticles xxxi) And, further: "Let me be so transformed in Thy beauty, that, being alike in beauty, we may see ourselves both in Thy beauty; so that one beholding the other, each may see his own beauty in the other, the beauty of both being Thine only, and mine absorbed in it." (Canticles xxxvi). Also the great Plotinus tells us: "If then a man sees himself become one with the One, he has in himself a likeness of the One, and if he passes out of himself as an image to its archtype, he has reached the end of his journey. This may be called the flight of the alone to the Alone." (Enneads, VI. 9.9.11). Mystics see the relation of the self and God as something like the relation between an image and its prototype, but never more than a likeness, never represented in full, but close enough to defy expression.

Bhakti and Jnāna are not really different. In the final stages, in the case of both, the identity with the individual entity does disappear, and Maharaj, in his usual direct and im-mediate approach, asks us to accept this true basis at once and totally reject the false one. He does not say that it is easy, but at the same time exhorts us not to keep chasing a mere shadow as the ideal. He wants us *to accept* our true stand *now,* firmly, with conviction, and let the shadow merge in the substance! If you keep chasing the shadow as the ideal, the ideal will always be receding from you, says he.

Lord Krishna points out in the Bhagvadgītā, shloka 10, chapter 10: "I give Buddhi Yoga, the Yoga of discrimination, to those ever-devout who worship Me with love, by means of which they come to Me." As the glory of God begins to dawn in the mind of the worshipper and he gets more and more involved in his love for God, Nature leads him to whatever is necessary for further progress. Maharaj says that the Gurū is always there ready with his grace; all that is required is the capacity, the required kind of receptivity, to accept it. All that is necessary is sincerity and determination. Nature does the rest according to the needs and circumstances of each case.

It would be interesting to examine in this context what two of the great Indian mystics — Jnaneshvara, fundamentally a Jnānī, and Tukarama, acknowledged as one of the greatest Bhaktas — have to say on the subject.

In his Jnaneshvari (XVIII 1130-1183), perhaps the greatest commentary yet done on the Bhagavadgītā, Jnaneshvara says:

"By the mirror of knowledge and devotion, he (the unitive mystic) is merged in Me, and has become one with Me . . . . .

as when a mirror is placed against a mirror, which mirror may be said to reflect what? . . . . He rejoices in Me even though he has become one with Me. . . ."

In the Jnaneshvari, and especially in his Amritanubhava, we see the greatness of Jnaneshvara as a philosopher. But it is really in his Abhanga * literature that we find him pouring out his heart in Bhakti. It is generally believed that Jnaneshvara, also known as Jnanadeva, being a Jnāni, did not suffer the pangs of separation from God which the Bhakta suffers. But there are quite a few of his early Abhangas which show that, like Tukarama and other Bhaktas, Jnaneshvara also did pine for his beloved God. He wails that in spite of being one with God, he is not able to see Him. "I pine after Thee," says he, "As a thirsty man longs for water." Then, in frustration, he says: "Let Thy will be done, for all my supplications have been useless."

Jnaneshvara goes into a poetic flight when he describes the attainment of bliss consequent on communion with God. "As I approached God, my intellect stood motionless and as I saw Him I became Himself . . ." (Abhanga 79). Then again: "Throughout all my experience I have been overwhelmed by silence. What shall I do if I cannot speak a word? Nivritti showed me God in my heart, and I have been enjoying each day a new aspect of Him" (Abhanga 76). And further, "Filled with God, within and without, as one goes to embrace Him, one becomes identified with Him. God cannot be warded off even if one so wills. Self-hood is at an end. As desire runs after God, God hides Himself. In a moment's time, however, He shows Himself when all desires become quiescent."

Jnaneshvara symbolizes within himself a unity not only of Jnāna and Bhakti but also Yoga in its various aspects. Being fully aware that it is impossible at the intellectual level to understand God's nature, or one's own true nature, he says: "The cool south wind cannot be made to drop like water from a wet piece of cloth; the fragrance of flowers cannot be tied by a string . . . the lustre of pearls cannot be made to fill a pitcher; the sky cannot be enclosed." (Abhanga

* Abhanga literature in Marathi comprises lyrical outpouring by Bhaktas in praise of God.

93.) To him the divine appears as the unity of man and woman; Shiva and Shakti are both merged in Him. True bliss, says Jnaneshvara, is to be found only in self-vision, and discribes it as follows. "He sees his own form present everywhere. He sees the reflection of form without form. *The seer vanishes, everywhere God is present.* There is neither any rising nor any setting of God. God alone *is*, and He enjoys his own happiness in His unitive experience. The invisible husband keeps awake in his bed without any partaker of it" (Abhanga 91).

According to Dr.R.D. Ranade, "Jnanadeva's philosophy preserves both the oneness and manyness of experience. His spiritual mysticism reconciles both monism and pluralism." He quotes from Macnicol the following significant words: "Not in the monism of Sankaracharya, nor in the dualism that is quite satisfied to remain two, but in the spiritual experience that transcends and includes them both, is peace to the found."

In contrast to Jnaneshvara, Tukarama's mystical career provides a typical instance of pure Bhakti. He undergoes unbelievable. sufferings and anxieties until, finally and suddenly, he has God-vision, or the self-vision, which transforms his weary life into one of light, freedom and total harmony. He describes his innermost experience in lyrical verse: "The whole world has now become alit and darkness is at an end. . . It is impossible to describe the bliss of unceasing illumination. . . God and self are now lying in the same bed. . . The whole world is filled with divine music. . . Both my exterior and interior are filled with divine bliss. . ." And finally, the highest experience of the mystic: "I gave birth to myself, and came out of my own womb; all my desires are at an end and my goal is achieved. . . . .all things have merged and disappeared into unicity. . . I do not see anything, and yet I see everything. I and mine have been removed from me. I talk without talking. I eat without eating. . . I do not need to be born and to die. *I am as I am.* *There is neither name nor form for me, and I am beyond both action and inaction.* . . ."Worshipping, Thou becomes an

* Mysticism in Maharashtra, page 179.

impossibility as Thou art identical with all the means of
worship. If I want to sing a song (of Thy praises) Thou art that
song. If I sound the cymbals Thou art the cymbals."

Tukarama's Abhangas are replete with mysticism. He says
that he would like his God not to be formless: "Be formless
for those who want Thee so, but for me do take on a form and
a name which I can love. . ." Later, however, Tukarama
establishes an identity between God and the devotee: "We
have now come to know Thy real nature. There is neither
saint nor God. There is no seed, how can there be fruit?
Everything is an illusion."

We have seen both Bhakti and Jnāna in action, and it is
clear that they are not separate paths for 'attaining' the
Ultimate. There is really no question of 'selecting' one or the
other. In the mystical experience the 'individual' is totally
annihilated, whatever the circumstances — that is to say,
whether the take-off stage was reached through devotion, or
through knowledge, or by a combination of both. The clear
conclusion is that so long as the idea of a separate entity with
independent doership remains, the mystical experience of
the universe being an illusion can not occur. Therefore, we
must accept the fact that *there never was, there never could
be a separate entity either to be bound or to be liberated.*

There are millions of human beings in the world, each
psyche being inclined by temperament towards that which
its physical composition (the particular combination of the
particular shade of each of the five elements and the three
attributes of Sattva, Rajas and Tamas) indicates. If this is
borne in mind, we would readily appreciate the widely
differing aptitudes of people desirous of knowing their true
nature. There are some psyches which, as Ramana Maharshi
used to say, are like dry wood-shavings or gunpowder that
need but one spark of the fire of knowledge from the lips of
the Guru to set them alight. While there are others so wet
that they are not capable of responding quickly even to a
blazing fire. And, of course, in between these outer
parameters exists the whole of world population.

In this set-up, would it not be ridiculous to talk of the
difference between Bhakti and Jnāna and which 'path' to

'choose'? And who is to 'choose'? When Maharaj asked the European visitor who was desirous of knowing the difference between devotion and knowledge, as to 'who' was asking the question, it was surely in this context. The entire process known as 'life', beginning with the 'birth' of a physical form and ending with its 'death', is part of the total functioning of consciousness, the relative manifesting of the Absolute Unmanifest. And the mystical experience, which takes place spontaneously in the very few cases, is part of this total functioning too. The fundamental question therefore is: Can the individual, an illusory entity, decide independently as by choice, that he wants to be 'liberated', that he must choose the method, i.e. Bhakti or Jnāna, and that he would make certain effort in that direction? No, he can not. Would it not be wiser for him and, incidentally, more practical too, to accept passively *what is* as part of the total functioning, and look at whatever happens in wondrous admiration of the working of Nature? The prompt but thoughtless reaction to this suggestion often is: If everyone adopts such a 'fatalistic' attitude, no one will work or make any progress. Maharaj's immediate answer to such a reaction is: Well, try it actually and see if Nature works that way. How long can you sit still without doing anything — ten minutes? This is where the physical and mental make-up of each psychosomatic apparatus comes in — it will work according to the way it is constructed, whether in the material field or in the spiritual.

There is an extremely important, though rather subtle, aspect of this matter which is often lost sight of. It is that spiritual development in each case, depending upon the make-up of each psyche, takes place spontaneously, and any deliberate efforts from the pseudo-entity would only create hazards and obstructions. When this fact is constantly kept in mind, one automatically keeps away from the greatest spiritual hazard i.e. the uprising of the ego. In the absence of a firm anchoring of the mind in the non-existence of an independent entity, the aspirants, whether following the path of Jnāna or Bhakti, would perhaps unwittingly begin thinking of themselves as privileged persons, superior not

only to those who in their view were the average misguided
individuals, but also in comparison to each other. Each
would consider his 'path' superior to the other's. But in
reality there is no difference between Jnāna and Bhakti. The
aspirant on the path of Jnāna, while listening to the words of
his Jnānī Guru, finds his eyes misting and his consciousness
almost in abeyance when the arrow of the Guru's words hits
the target. So is the Bhakta totally lost in the devotional song
and dance of the Guru and his fellow disciples. Can there be
any real difference between the two?

We seem to have arrived at a working formula on the
subject. *What is the individual to do?* The only thing one can
do is always to keep in mind the fact that an independent
entity cannot exist, and also the fact that the entire
manifestation is the functioning of consciousness in which
each one of us has one's allotted role to play and, finally, to
accept whatever happens within that total functioning with a
sense of wondrous admiration. The one thing that remains
thereafter is not any 'practising' as a deliberate effort, but
merely to let our true understanding deeply impregnate our
very being, passively and patiently, so that all illusions and
obstructions gradually fall off by themselves.   ●●

The Whole Truth

In its state of perfection, of total Awareness
IT is unaware of its awareness;
Then consciousness stirs into a moan of *Aum,*
and the dream - creation begins.
IT is conscious of *being,*
IT exults in this beingness.
Immersed in the love of *I-am-ness,*
IT expresses itself in duality.
Through union of twin aspects male-female,
Through the five elements —
Space-air-fire-water and earth,
Through the three Gunas —
Sattva-Rajas-Tamas —
IT manifests itself in duration.
In *dreamed* space-time
IT manifests as phenomena,
Creating millions of forms,
Breathing into them the life-force
And the all-pervading immanent consciousness;
Through these forms, in joyous self-love
functions consciousness as Prajnā.
The sentient beings, mere images,
Thus conceived — wonder of wonders! —
Perceive one another as objects,
    assuming subjectivity for oneself,
Each, in magnificent illusion,
Sees oneself as an entity separate,
With judgement and volition independent.
Each forgets his unlimited potential

as noumenal Absolute, accepts
His limited identity as an appearance,
A mere phenomenon;
Takes delivery of the functioning of Prajñā
As his own personal actions,
Binds himself in illusory bondage,
And 'suffers' pain and pleasure!
Comes then, the merciful Gurū,
Full of Grace and Light divine,
And shows him what it really is —
That which he thinks he is:
Nothing more than the speck of sperm
Impregnated in the mother's womb,
In which is latent the light of sentience
I-am-ness, the Consciousness that he is.
Given names in thousands,
Rama, Krishna, Ishwara, Brahman,
The same *I-am-ness* it is;
The light of Consciousness, Mahāmāyā,
In magnificent illusion, illudes
Its own nature and leads itself astray.
Until the Gurū says: Halt, see yourself
As you are, in your true glory.
On your original state of timeless,
Absolute noumenality, has appeared
Like a temporary illness, the body-cum-consciousness,
Spontaneously, sans cause or reason,
      as part of Prajñā-ic functioning.
It works out its allotted duration
Until, just as spontaneously it disappears —
      and consciousness, no longer conscious of itself,
Merges in Awareness — no one is born, no one dead.
Says Nisargadatta Maharaj
In terms simple and direct:
What were you before you acquired the body?
Go back to the source; be still, and *then*
Will the seeker disappear and
Into the seeking merge.
No longer aware of awareness, in

Wholeness, in unicity, without duality *I am.*
With insight and intuition, with
   deep conviction, simple to apprehend,
This-That-Is is beyond the bounds of intellect.
Only the objective and the phenomenal —
   presence or absence — can the Intellect grasp.
But *what-I-Am* is neither presence nor absence;
Absence of the presence of presence,
Absence of the presence of absence,
Is *what-I-Am.*

Glossary

Advaita

Non-dualism: the doctrine of monism which contends that only the Ultimate Principle *(Brahman)* has existence and all phenomenal existence is illusion (Māyā). It is the most important branch of Vedānta. (neg. participle *a*, without + *dvaita*, dualism, twoness, *dvi*, two).

Ākāsha

Sky, the expanse of vacuity (fr. prep. *ā*, to + *kāsha*, appearance). Ether as an element.

Ānanda

Bliss, joy, one of the three elements of the Ultimate Principle — *sat*, *chit* and *ānanda* (prep. *ā*, to + *nand*, to rejoice, be pleased).

Antahkaraṇa

The internal doer, the psyche (compounded of *antar*, internal + *karaṇa*, sense-organ, √*kar* to do, make). Hence mind in the collective sense, including intelligence *(buddhi)*, ego *(aham)* and mind *(manas)*.

Apāra

Limitless, not having the opposite shore (*a*, negative prefix + *pāra*, across).

Ārati

Worship in praise of a deity (*ār*, *āryanti*, to praise).

Āsana

Sitting, posture; one of the eight stages in the practice of Yoga (√*as*, to sit).

Ātmā, Ātman

The soul, self *(ātm*, belonging to oneself). Ātman is beyond the *gunas* of Prakṛiti — *sattva, rajas* and *tamas*. Ātmā is pure awareness.

Ātmajnāna

Knowledge of the self (*ātm*, self + *jnāna*, knowledge).

Avadhūta

One who has shaken off all worldly feelings and obligations, philosopher (*dhū*, to shake off + *ta* suffix).

Avatār

Incarnation, descent of a deity (*ava*, off, down + √tr, to pass across, to descend).

Aum

This word and its sound denote *Brahman*, the Ultimate Principle. *Aum* is the symbol of the Supreme Self. It is believed to be the most sacred Mantra. The significance of *Aum* is discussed in Mandukya Upanishad in terms of supreme consciousness. The letter *a* stands for consciousness of the world of senses, *u* stands for the subconscious mind and *m* stands for *Prajñā*, the state which is beyond mind. Also called Pranava, it is accepted as a symbol of God.

Avyakta

The unmanifest (neg. part. *a*, un + *vyakta*, manifest). It is the opposite of *vyakta*.

Bhajan

Devotional practice, prayer (*bhaj*, to adore).

Bhakti, Bhakta

Devotion, adoration as a way of salvation (*bhaj*, to adore, worship, love). *Bhakta* is one who is devoted to his adored deity.

Bhoga

Experiencing worldly pleasures as well as sorrows (*bhuj*, to enjoy, to endure).

Brahmā

One of the gods of the Hindu Trinity — *Brahmā*, the creator, *Vishnu* the preserver and *Shiva*, or *Maheshwara*, the annihilator. (*brh*, to increase, to create) *Brahmā* creates and increases his creation.

Brahman

The Absolute, the Ultimate Reality, which is self-existent (*brh*, to grow, increase). Its three attributes are: being (*sat*), consciousness (*chit*) and bliss (*ananda*). Brahman is not an object of worship, but of meditation and knowledge.

Chetanā

Consciousness, the inner awakening (*chit*, to perceive).

Chidākāsh

The expanse of inner awareness (*chit*, to perceive + *ākāsh*, expanse, sky).

Chit

Universal consciousness (*chit*, to perceive).

Chitta

Individual consciousness. It is a combination of Purusha and Prakriti — consciousness and matter. Chitta comprises all levels of mind —

objective consciousness, subjective consciousness and the unconscious.

Darshana

Viewing, seeing, meeting (*dars*, to see). Darshana also implies a philosophical system that gives insight into the Reality. Also written as Darshan.

Dharma

That which sustains, a firm code of conduct and duty (*dhri*, to hold, bear, support). In a metaphysical sense Dharma means laws of Nature that sustain the operation of the universe, inherent properties of elements, like the Dharma of fire is to burn.

Dhyāna

Meditation (*dhyāi*, to think of, to meditate).

Guṇas

Attributes, qualities. The three attributes of the cosmic substance (Prakriti) are: *sattva, rajas* and *tamas* (√*grah*, single thread or strand of a cord). Guṇas are fundamental attributes of all physical, mental and psychic manifestations in universe.

Guṇatīta

Beyond the Guṇas (*guṇa*, attribute +*atita*, past, beyond). d).

Gūru, Gūru Pūrnima

Preceptor, spiritual preceptor (*gurū*, large, weighty, superior). Gurū Pūrnima is the festive day on which the disciples re-dedicate themselves to their preceptor. It occurs once a year on a date when the moon is full (Pūrṇimā).

Īshwara

The supreme lord (*ish*, to be master + *vara*, supreme). The word stands for God as the lord and master of the universe.

Japa

Muttering of a certain Mantra as invocation to a deity, generally on a rosary.

Jīva, Jīvātman

The individual soul (*jiv*, to live). According to Vedānta Jīva comes into being as a result of false identification of the Ātmān with the body, the senses and the mind. Ātman + doership is Jīva. Without doership Ātman is Supreme Awareness.

Jnāna, Jnānī

Jnāna is knowledge, specially the higher knowledge derived from meditation (*jnā*, to know). Jnānī is the knower. Also pronounced as Gnana and Gnanī.

Kāma

Desire, love, wish (*kam*, to wish, desire, long for). The god of love is known as Kāmadeva.

Karma, Karman

Action, especially responsible action — good or evil. The principle of causality, popularly known as the law of cause and effect (kar, to-do).

Līlā

Play, sport, the cosmos looked upon as a divine play (la, play). Līlā does not represent the Absolute Truth of Brahman. It is only partial truth, not different from untruth.

Mahā, Mahat

Great (mahā, great). Mahat stands for the great principle, Cosmic Intelligence.

Mahadākāsh

The great expanse of existence, the universe of matter and energy (mahat, great + ākāsh, expanse, sky).

Mahārāj

An honorific term used for spiritual preceptors and kings. Other words qualified by Mahā are Mahāvākya, Mahātattva, Mahākāvya etc.

Mahātmā

An honorific term used for spiritual teachers (mahā, great + ātmā. soul), indicating great soul.

Māhasamādhī

A term used for the death of a spiritical preceptor, indicating that by dropping the physical body he has attained the great and the final Samādhī, a superconscious state from which there is no return.

Mahāvākya

The sublime pronouncement (mahā, great + vach, word, sound; vākya speech, sentence).

Maheshwara

Name of Shiva, one of the gods of the Hindu Trinity. (mah, great + Īshwara, lord — the great lord).

Mana, Manas

The mind as organ of cognition, perception and understanding (man, to think, conjecture). Its main functions are: perception, attention, selection and rejection.

Manana

Meditation, reflection, the act of thinking (man, to think). Manana is discriminative understanding through thinking.

Mantra

Instrument of thought; hymn, incantation. Ideal sounds visualized as letters and vocalized as syllables. Constant repetition of a Mantra produces the desired specific results, by unfolding the latent psychic and occult faculties.

Māyā

Delusion, the veiling power discussed in the Vedānta philosophy. It is the finitizing principle which creates forms in the formless; it conceals the real and projects the unreal (*mā*, creating illusions). Māyā ends where pure mental awareness begins.

Moksha

Emancipation, liberation from worldly existence (*muc*, to set loose, free, release). One who is emancipated is the Mukta.

Mumukshu

One who is anxious for liberation from mundane existence (*muc*, to set loose, free).

Mumukshattva

Earnest desire for liberation from the world and knowledge of the truth (*muc*, to free).

Nāda

Loud sound (*nad*, sound, roaring).

Nāma Mantra

A Mantra based on the name of a deity.

Nāmarūpa

The phenomenal world of name and form (*nama*, name + *rūpa*, form).

Namaskār

Bowing in obesience or homage (*namas*, to bow).

Nididhyāsana

Profound and repeated meditation (*ni* prefix + *dhyāyati*, to meditate).

Nirguna

The unconditioned, without the three attributes — *sattva*, *rajas* and *tamas* (*nir*, without + *guna*, attributes).

Nisarga

Natural state, (preposition *ni* + *srij*, to create, to let flow uninterrupted).

Nivritti

Stopping of the ramifications of mind, eschewing the worldly concerns (*nir*, without + *vritti*, √*vart*, to turn, revolve; the rut of life). It is opposite of Pravritti which means indulgence in worldly life.

Parā

Beyond, distant, ulterior (*par*, to pass). Parama is the superlative form of *parā*; it means most distant, most excellent, the supreme.

Parama Brahman

The Supreme Spirit (compounded of *parama*, most excellent +

Brahman, the Ultimate Reality). Also written as Parābrahman.

Paramākāsh

Limitless expanse of the sky, the timeless and spaceless Supreme Reality (*parama*, highest, greatest + *ākāsh*, the void, sky). The Ultimate Absolute.

Paramārtha

The greatest good, the Sublime Truth (*parama* the highest, greatest + *artha*, purpose, knowledge).

Paramātman, Paramātmā

The Supreme Self (*parama*, superlative of *para* + *ātman*, the self).

Parāvritti

The highest conduct (*parā* the highest, + *vritti* fr. *vart*, to turn, revolve). Vritti stands for course of action, especially moral conduct.

Prajñā

Unselfconscious knowledge, pure awareness (*prajin*, wise, *pra*, high + *jna*, to know). Prajñā stands for the higher consciousness. Also pronounced as Pragñā.

Prakṛiti

Cosmic Substance, Primal Nature, the original uncaused cause of phenomenal existence, which is formless, limitless and all-pervading (*pra*, before, first + *kr.*, to make). Prakṛiti comprises three Guṇas — *sattva*, *rajas* and *tamas* and also the five elements (tattvas) — *ākāsha*, *vāyu*, *tejas*, *āpas* and *pṛithivi*. Prakṛiti means that which existed before anything was produced.

Prāṇa

The breath of life, the vital principle (*pra*, before + *aṇa*, breath).

Premākāsh

Limitless love (*prem*, love + *ākāsh*, sky, expanse).

Pṛithivi, Pṛthivi

Earth as one of the five elements, the principle of solidarity. Its special property is odour (*gandh*); (*prathu*, to spread, extend.) Pṛithivi is a vast extension.

Pūjā

Worship, adoration (*pū*, *pūyati*, *pūta*, to purify). Worship purifies. *Pūjya* is one deserving Pūjā.

Pūrṇimā

Full moon night (*pūrṇa*, full; participle of *par*, to fill).

Purusha

The Cosmic Spirit, the eternal and efficient cause of creation that gives consciousness to all manifestation of matter (prakṛiti). It is the background of all that is or shall be. Also used for male human being (etymology uncertain).

Rāga

Desire, attachment (*ra(n)j*, to be coloured).

Rajas

Motivity, activity, energy, (*ra(n)j*, to be coloured, affected, moved). One of the three Gunas of Prakriti — *sattva, rajas* and *tamas*. In Yoga it refers to the activating aspect of Nature without which the other constituents could not manifest their inherent qualities.

Rāja Yoga

Abstract meditation; propounded by Patanjali in his Yoga Sutra. (√ *ra(n)j*, coloured, radiant). Raja Yoga emphasizes control of mind and suppressing its modifications for awakening pure consciousness.

Sadchit

Truth and perception (*sat*, true being + *chit*, perception). Also written as *Saccid*. Saccidānanda (*sat + chit + ananda*) refers to the three attributes of Brahman — being, consciousness and bliss.

Sadgurū

The true spiritual teacher (*sat*, true + *gurū*, teacher).

Sādhaka, Sādhanā

The practice that leads to the goal is *sādhanā*, (*sidh, sādhati*, to attain, to succeed, accomplish). *Sādhaka* is one who practises a Sādhanā. *Siddha* is one who has accomplished, reached the goal. *Siddhi* is the accomplishment.

Sādhu

An ascetic, holy man (*Sādh* to go straight, also earnest wish).

Saguṇa

With the attributes, manifested condition with the *gunas* (*sa*, with + *guṇa*, attribute). The Bhakti cult conceives the Supreme Absolute as having qualities like love, mercy etc. God to them is *saguṇa*. The Vedāntic concept of the Supreme Absolute is *nirguṇa*, without or beyond attributes, *gunatita*.

Samādhi ·

Superconscious state, profound meditation (*sam*, together + *a*, to + *dhi*, placing, putting together). Samādhi is a Yogic practice in which the seeker (*sādhaka*) becomes one with his object of meditation, thus attaining unqualified bliss. Samādhi is also used for the memorial of a saint; it could be a brick or stone construction or a pillar. Mahā-samādhi stands for the death of a saint, who is believed to have attained a permanent superconscious state on the dissolution of his physical body.

Sansāra

The round of existence (*sam*, together + *sara*, flowing, *sar*, to flow). Sansāra is the passage of soul in the cycle of births and deaths. Also pronounced as Samsāra.

Sanyāsin, Sanyāsī

One who has abandoned all worldly concern (*sam* prefix + *nyāsa*, abandoning, laying aside). Also written as Samyāsin.

Sattva

Being, existence, reality (*sat*, real + abstract formative *tva*). One of the three constituents of the Cosmic Substance — *sattva, rajas* and *tamas*. Sattva is the quality of purity and goodness. It stands for equilibrium and manifests itself as light.

Shakti

Power, energy, capacity (fr. √ *sak*, to be strong). Shakti is portrayed as the female aspect of the Ultimate Principle and deified as the wife of Shiva.

Shravaṇa

Hearing, listening attentively (*sru*, to hear). It is the first stage of self-culture, followed by *manana, chintana* and *nididhyāsana* on what one has heard.

Svarūpa

One's own form, nature, character (*sva*, one's own + *rūpa*, form).

Tamas

Darkness, inertia, passivity, restraint. One of the three constituents of the Cosmic Substance. The other two are *sattva* and *rajas*.

Tattva

The true essence, truth, reality (pronoun *tad*, that + abstract suffix *tva*). Thatness.

Vairāgya

Right dispassion, indifference to worldly concerns (*vi*, apart, away, without + *rāga*, desire, attachment). Vairāgya is the opposite of Raga. It is renunciation of all desires.

Veda

Revealed knowledge, a generic name for the most ancient sacred literature of the Hindus (*vid*, to know). *Vidyā* is knowledge, *Vidvān* is a learned man. There are four collections of the Vedic hymns: 1. Rgveda, hymns to gods, 2. Sāmaveda, priests' chants, 3. Yajurveda, sacrificial formulae and 4. Atharvaveda, mainly magical chants.

Vedānta

Literally, the end of Vedas (*veda* + *anta*, end). Vedānta is one of the six schools of Hindu philosophy. Advaita Vedānta is the most well-known branch of Vedānta.

Vishnū

One of the gods of the Hindu trinity — Brahmā, Vishnū and Shiva. Vishnū is the preserver.

Vishvarūpa

The muli-formed universe (*vis*, to pervade + *rūpa*, form). Vishvarūpa is many-coloured, variegated universe..

Vritti

Mode of life and conduct, mental modifications (*vart*, to turn around, revolve).

Vyakta, Vyakti

Manifested matter, the evolved Nature (*vi*, apart, away + *akta*, passive participle of *anj*, to annoint). Hence the annointed, evolved, manifested product is Vyakti.

Yoga, Yogi

Yoga means joining together (*yuj*, to yoke, to join). Yoga is a method by which consciousness is disconnected from the entanglement with mind and the manifested world. It is a unique psychiatric-psychological system leading to enlightenment and liberation. An adept in Yoga is called Yogi.